T0156996

# PRO BONO PUBLICO

Policing In The 21ˢᵗ Century

BY CAPTAIN ROGER B. HOULE, JR. (RET.)

Order this book online at www.trafford.com
or email orders@trafford.com

Most Trafford titles are also available at major online book retailers.

I express many opinions in this book. Although I like my opinions they do not supersede your
department's rules and regulations, nor do they supersede state and federal laws. The views
of the author are not necessarily the views of the East Providence, RI Police Department
nor of any other agency or person mentioned in this book. I hope you enjoy this book and
that you find it helpful, regardless of what role you play in law enforcement. Thank you.

Print information available on the last page.

ISBN: 978-1-4907-9023-7 (sc)
ISBN: 978-1-4907-9024-4 (hc)
ISBN: 978-1-4907-9025-1 (e)

Library of Congress Control Number: 2018909730

Scripture quotations marked NASB are taken from the New American
Standard Bible®, Copyright © 1960, 1962, 1963, 1968, 1971, 1972, 1973,
1975, 1977, 1995 by The Lockman Foundation. Used by permission.

*Trafford rev. 08/16/2018*

 www.trafford.com
North America & international
toll-free: 1 888 232 4444 (USA & Canada)
fax: 812 355 4082

# DEDICATION

I dedicate this book to my four children; Randy, Kimberly, Amanda and Roger III, who are the loves of my life and have always been there for me, in the good times and the bad.

# CONTENTS

# PRELUDE

My name is Roger B. Houle Jr., and I have been involved with law enforcement for many decades. I proudly served with the police department of the city of East Providence, Rhode Island, for twenty-four years. During that time, I served at various ranks and in various assignments, starting my career as a patrol officer working on the street. As a detective, I was assigned to the vice unit, major crimes unit, and crime scene investigation unit. Throughout my career, I was blessed to achieve the ranks of detective, sergeant, lieutenant, and eventually, captain. As captain, I served as the division commander of both the patrol division and the detective division (not at the same time). I was the third-ranking officer of the department while serving at this rank. I preface this book with a brief background of my career to demonstrate that my experience in law enforcement was diverse. I feel it gives me great insight into the law enforcement profession and what I am trying to relate to the reader of this book.

This book is to provide guidance not only for those in the law enforcement profession but also for those who may be considering a career in law enforcement. It is also geared toward a citizen who has no aspiration of being a police officer but who wants some insight as to what your police officers are dealing with on a daily basis, and how to help them better achieve their mission.

I am not going to cite multiple authors, their studies, their findings, their theses, their hypothesis, or the like. I am not going to list numerous footnotes because if something from someone else is worth mentioning, I will give them the credit at the time and not waste your time, flipping through footnotes, as if most of you do anyway. In the event I quote something that you feel is an original thought and I don't give credit where credit is due, please send me the documentation, and I will gladly correct it in the next printing. I sometimes use Internet resources for quick reference because we all know if it is on the Internet, it must be true.

When I relay personal stories of the women and men I so proudly served with, my sisters and brothers, I will refer to them at the rank they achieved at the time of this writing, not necessarily and most often not the rank they were at the time when the incident occurred. I have been told I am very frank, and you may pick up on this as you read on. As a Christian, my career was influenced by my faith, and I thank God for having been given the gift of being a public servant for so many years.

# INTRODUCTION

At the time of this writing, the words *terrorism* and *terrorist* have definitely moved up the ladder on the list of words used frequently by the average American. After the horrific attacks of 9/11, we as a country have responded by declaring war on terrorism. While we fight this global war on terror, how are we dealing with those who terrorize our nation on a daily basis and have been doing so long before September 11? These are people who prey on the innocent daily. They are just as cowardly and just as deadly as any other terrorist but don't often get the public notoriety. "Who is this?" you ask. Criminals!

One of the biggest problems facing this country today, as it has been since its inception, is the impact criminals have on our society. Criminals prey upon our citizen's daily, and the overall cost in lives and property is much greater than from some isolated, albeit horrific, attack. Who do we count on to protect us against this onslaught of crime? Your local law enforcement agency—that's who. The criminal justice system is a very complex system composed of many groups and facets. It is a great system, but at two in the morning when some thug is trying to break into your home, whom do you call? You call the only agency that still answers the telephone at two in the morning—the police department. At least I hope they still answer the telephone because, as this book will discuss, the role of the police officer is facing many challenges as we enter into the twenty-first century.

This book will look at the role of police officers in today's society. Our officers have been known by many names over the years: lawman, marshal, trooper, sheriff, constable, and guard. They are also referred to by their slang names as well—copper, cop, pig, 5-0, fuzz—and the list goes on. Regardless what they have been called over the centuries, the job is basically the same. This book will examine how this role is being muddied as we enter this technological, politically correct age. I hope to provide you with some insight into the law enforcement profession based on my years of service as a sworn police officer.

Whether you are in law enforcement, considering a career in law enforcement, or just a concerned citizen, I urge you to read on. I will not bore you with studies, statistics, or specifics but provide you with my own insight into the profession, the challenges it faces, and some ways to make it better. The book is designed to stand the test of time to hopefully be valuable to many generations of law enforcement officers yet to come. This book will not focus on the various technologies or specialized techniques in law enforcement. As we all know, technology is rapidly advancing, and law enforcement is no exception. I am going to try and relate to you how police officers can individually be their best, how administrators can be their best, and how civilians can enhance their local law enforcement agency. There are many changes facing police officers in the twenty-first century. Many of these changes are good and have made the job safer and have increased the ability to solve crime. Some of these changes, however, are very detrimental to the profession. Hopefully, a part of this book will point out these problematic areas and provide viable solutions.

There are many great police stories that come out of the metropolitan hubs of the nations, but most of us in law enforcement don't work there. We work for average departments that lend themselves to knowing all the officers whom you work with, and after a short time, you become familiar with your entire jurisdiction. Although I use the term *average*, there should be nothing average about you or about your department. You should be the best, and many of the citizens who live in your community really think you are the best. The perception that you are hated and mistrusted by the citizens is a falsehood, perpetuated by a small group of individuals who, in fact, don't like you or what you stand for. This is the group who want to muddy the mission of law enforcement to pursue their own agenda, and in some cases, they are succeeding.

For those of you in or planning a future career in law enforcement, I hope this book will show you ways to make your job fun and successful. This book will provide an overview of policing and how you can become a better police officer. For those of you not in the law enforcement profession or have any aspirations of doing so, I hope to relate to you what the police officers who are protecting you daily are facing on a daily basis and how you can help them in their mission. As a concerned citizen, you have a great impact on your local law enforcement agency, and you should be involved.

# CHAPTER 1

## QUALIFICATIONS OF A POLICE OFFICER

B ecoming a police officer never crossed my mind when I was young. The first inkling I ever had toward this career was when I was sixteen years old. While at work one day, I could see that the state police had set up a radar trap across the street from my workplace. I pointed this out and made a smart comment about this to one of my coworkers. This coworker was a ranking member of an organized crime family who, at this time, was on a work release program (I was not). After my remark, he scolded me, telling me that I should always respect the police. He had nothing but compliments toward the police, telling me how honorable they were in spite of his past dealings. He went on to say that it was a great profession and something I should consider for a career. Needless to say, I was a bit speechless.

After this learning experience, I started to pay closer attention to just what police officers did, especially now that I had my driver's license. Through my teenage years, there were a couple of officers who really stood out to me as class acts. They looked and acted in a professional manner. They were human; you could talk to them. They were not pushovers, but they certainly used discretion. These officers were Russ Fontaine from the Lincoln PD and Joe Connors from the neighboring community of Cumberland.

Based on my experiences and my lecture, I applied to one police department when I was eighteen years old, came out number one on the test, but never got hired. I tried again for the same department a couple of years later, and again, I was not hired. (Later in life, I found out my Dad was using his connections to keep me safe, not hired.) The next time this idea crossed my path was when I was twenty-two, and my teenage friend Ralph Ezovksi applied for the East Providence Police Department and got hired. Our cohort Joe Broadmeadow and I said why not, and we applied. We were both hired and on the job within a year. The interesting part was, coming from the Blackstone Valley area, that none of us even knew where the East Providence Police Department was at first. For my dear friend Cpl. Rolland Grant, it really wasn't a Blackstone Valley conspiracy, and none of us knew the personnel director who happened to be from the Blackstone Valley region as well.

Who is qualified to serve as a law enforcement officer? You might have seen an advertisement in a local newspaper:

> Help wanted: There are openings now for policemen. Good pay and benefits. Qualifications: white males, over 5'10" tall, no eyeglasses, no experience necessary; training is provided.

Early in the twentieth century, that is. Now if you ever saw an ad such as this today, it would certainly draw some attention as it should. If this is the current hiring standard, the unwritten rule still being used as hiring criteria, then you have problems. Although each department will have various criteria for hiring—sex, race, size, corrective lenses, sexual orientation, along with many other criteria used in the past—it should have no bearing on a candidate's qualifications today.

What are the qualifications? Being a police officer is not just a job; it is a mind-set and lifestyle. You are going to have to think in ways the average citizen does not. You are going to have to look at situations with a slanted, suspicious perception. You are going to literally see blood, guts, and gore. You will see human depravity at its worst. You are going to have to make split-second decisions that will then be scrutinized by others for many years to follow. You will have to act based on what is just, not on what is popular. You are going to be working when most others are not— weekends, holidays, nights, and during extreme weather conditions. You are going to be called upon to use force, maybe even deadly force, to protect the people you serve. As Lt. Col. Dave Crossman pointed out in one of his seminars, "When people naturally run away from a dangerous situation, you are going to be the one who instinctively runs into it."

With this in mind, who is qualified to serve as a police officer?

Anyone who realizes what the job involves, is physically and mentally able to perform it, and still wants to put their life at risk for society may be qualified. I say "may be qualified" because there are some who want to work in law enforcement for the wrong reasons.

Having read this, is the job really for you? Knowing this, though you have no intentions of going into law enforcement, are you as a citizen giving your local police officers the respect and support that they need and deserve? If you are not sure, please read on.

# HIRING PRACTICES

One of the most important aspects of having a good police department is the hiring practices that are in place. Most municipalities will have written guidelines setting the minimum qualifications and the acceptable procedures to be followed throughout the hiring practice. Proper screening of applicants for your law enforcement agency is vital. Each candidate needs to be screened physically, mentally and, in my opinion, a thorough background check into their character. You want to make sure you are getting people who want to be police officers for the right reasons and who will be able to endure and thrive in a police environment.

When I applied for the job, I took a written examination. Those who passed the written test went on to a physical agility test, followed by a psychological examination. If you successfully completed these and then ranked high enough, a background check was then done. Successful candidates were then ranked on a list based on their overall performance and selected as vacancies occurred. Most municipalities will maintain these lists for a time; ours was two years.

The first major change to this procedure was under Chief Winquist. He reversed this order by doing the physical agility test first. This immediately eliminated those who were not physically qualified. It also saved the city money as it could be done in-house using our own officers to monitor the tests at a minimal cost. After this, a written examination was done, which required the cost of an outside testing agency. By eliminating the first round of candidates, the cost for the written test was reduced. Those who passed the written exam based on numerical standing went on to the psychological examination. Once that was completed, a list of eligible candidates was formulated, and then officers were assigned to do background checks on the candidates. Chief Winquist also implemented posting the names of the candidates in-house. This frequently resulted in either positive or negative feedback from officers who had dealt with these individuals in the past.

The background check is by far the most important step in getting excellent officers. It is nice to know everyone is smart, physically able, and mentally sound, but the background of a person's character tells the true story of the candidate. This is only achieved through a thorough background check. I would like to emphasize *THOROUGH*. This is not "call the old boss and get the boilerplate" line "Great employee. I hate to see them leave."

The investigator then writes up the report, and the candidate is on the list to possibly become the next officer working in your community. They could be your partner, and your life will depend upon them. What if the previous employer told the investigator what they really wanted to say?

- "A cop? (As they laugh) Based on everything I saw, I can't believe this person wants to be a police officer."
- "He has been a nightmare the whole time he was employed here."
- "You're going to give her a gun with that temper? Good luck."

If you don't ask the right people the right questions, you are not going to get the real answers from past employers. You first need to get a release from the candidate, allowing previous employers to provide full disclosure. If the candidate is reluctant to sign such a release, that should be a red flag right from the start. Even with a release, in the era of lawsuits and political correctness, you may still get boiler-plate responses. These interviews should also be conducted by trained investigators, not office administrators or junior officers on light duty. Trained investigators are going to know when they are getting a boiler-plate answer and will go a little further, interviewing coworkers, requesting personnel files, etc. You need to speak with employers, neighbors, friends, and family. You also need to do a complete financial on them, just as if they were applying for a loan.

Chief Winquist had a very thorough process in place, but Chief Gary Dias added to this, and in my opinion, his was one of the best candidate-screening components I saw throughout my career. It was cost-effective, and it provided for multiple levels of candidate screening. It focused on a multilevel background check. He created a panel of seven officers to conduct in-house interviews to clarify any questions that may have come up during the background checks. The panel was very balanced with liberals and conservatives (yes, there are liberals in police work). The panel would ask the candidate to clarify any gray areas of the background check that had arisen. A vote would then be taken. Most often the candidate was able to clarify any issue and continued on in the hiring process. Infrequently, there were some who had something of concern in their past, which would eliminate them from the hiring process. As a check and balance, the city had its own personnel board that could accept or reject our panel's recommendations.

Although there were occasions the panel voted unanimously to keep a candidate, there was never an instance of the panel voting unanimously to eliminate a candidate, except once. It was regarding a candidate who had some questions from the past, which had raised some concerns. Compared with the myriad of other issues the panel had examined during the hiring processes, these were on the minor side. It was, however, the persona of the individual while answering our questions that aroused the sixth sense that police officers have. We can't use our sixth sense in a court of law, but all good cops have it. After the interview, the candidate was unanimously eliminated with very little discussion before the vote. The candidate was then able to argue this decision, and our decision was reversed by the personnel board that then allowed the candidate to have a final interview with the city manager and the command staff. Still bothered about his demeanor during this final interview, I briefly went over the application again and saw that Spanish, spoken moderately, was listed by the candidate as a second language. My Spanish at the time was very crude, but when it came to my turn to interview him during this final session, I spoke to him in Spanish, seeking responses. It was amazing to see that the candidate was unable to communicate at all in Spanish. The candidate could not even list basic items—such as telephone, car— when asked. Not only did this get rid of a potential problem, but it also demonstrated the need to go deeper and not take what was listed at face value. It also reinforced that sixth sense. We were a very diverse-minded group of officers by design for balance, yet we all had the same conclusion. As a police officer, don't ignore that sixth sense. Don't try and make it a probable cause but certainly examine the situation deeper when your sixth sense is aroused.

The question also comes up regarding the educational background of officer candidates. When I first applied for the job, most officers did not have a college degree. Many had attended college, often in an unrelated field, but few had earned their degree. Once hired, officers were encouraged to get their degree in criminal justice, and there were financial incentives for doing so. What was common was that most officers had military experience. As time passed, the hiring criteria changed, requiring candidates to have a minimum of an associate's degree before being eligible to take the examination. (Active military time was still accepted in lieu of a college degree.) At that time, I was a proponent of requiring all candidates to have a minimum of an associate's degree before being eligible to apply. It was a cost-saving measure for the city, and I, like many others, thought we were getting the best candidates. After observing this for almost forty years, I have definitely changed my mind. My peers, most of whom did not have degrees when they were hired, went on to become exceptional officers. Most continued their education, some even getting law degrees. What did we have that someone right out of college did not? Life skills. Academia is great, but without any work experience, you cannot tell how someone will be in a work environment. You don't have that former employer or coworker to interview to get a feel for the candidate. Many of the officers I mentioned above had some pretty diverse jobs and life experiences before becoming police officers. Those skills carried over into their job as police officers. Someone who has spent four years in college simply does not have this opportunity. I also noticed that most of the officers who earned their degree after being sworn in remained with our department until they were eligible for retirement. Unfortunately, this does not seem to be the case nowadays with officers bouncing from job to job, much like the corporate world. I can't say if it is from the lack of work experience or a culture promoted by colleges and universities or simply a generational culture. What I can say is don't limit your pool of candidates by making a college degree a requirement. You want to get the absolute best candidates for your police force, and not all of them have college degrees.

In summation, spend a lot of resources, both time and money, on your hiring practices. I will emphasize again. Have a TRAINED INVESTIGATOR do a THOROUGH BACKGROUND CHECK on ALL your potential officers. In the long run, you are going to get good, qualified individuals who will serve as excellent police officers. Spending the time and money up front will save a lot of time and money for legal expense down the road if someone who has issues slips through the cracks.

I have included some photographs from our academy class. I have to mention that Lt. Ernie Wilkinson was by far one of my great inspirations in my law enforcement career, although on the first day of the academy, when we all saw him standing silent in his full dress uniform, we all agreed that we were going to be in for three months of hell. How wrong we were. We soon found out that he was our greatest ally and taught us the meaning of camaraderie.

East Providence Police Graduating Class
RI Municipal Police Academy, 1979
Walter Barlow, Ernie Wilkinson (Class Commandant
RIDEM) Robert Pacheco, James Reddington, Donald Dubois,
Christopher Gilfillan, Stanley Chin, Roger Houle

Above with my classmates Thomas Mooney, Cranston PD, and Lester Newell, RIDEM; below with my friend and fellow officer Ralph Ezovski

With Lt. Ernest Wilkinson, Rhode Island Department of Environmental Management and below, my classmates on our first day with a police cruiser

# A POLICE OFFICER'S MIND-SET

I talk about having fun. Fun, you say. How can you do one of the most dangerous jobs in the world and have fun? It's easy if you love your job and do it as a professional. If you are not having fun being a police officer, you need to either change your attitude or quit. Yes, quit. You might not be in your right profession. Every department has those officers who fail to realize they are in the wrong profession. The longer you stay doing something you are not happy with, the longer you are hurting yourself. You are denying yourself a career in a field where your gifts and talents could be used to their full potential and where you would be happy. But just as important, by remaining in the police profession, you are an obstacle and danger to those officers who work with you.

Just because an officer's lifestyle may be different than the average citizen does not mean police officers should live the job, quite the contrary. Your priorities in life should be your spirituality first, your family second, and then your career last. If you get the first two right, your job will become much more fulfilling. As a Christian, I know God will never forsake me. From Him, I have everything. My family is the first responsibility He has given me. Family will be there for me, and you, long after the job is over, and your family is depending on you now. Will sacrifices have to be made among the three? Yes, they will. Are you going to get every Sunday off to attend church? I don't think so. Are you going to miss some family events because of something going on at work? Yes, you will. Are you going to put your job constantly above your family? You better not.

I remember vividly several years ago at a detective's roll call. Two officers were commenting on how you will never get to enjoy your children, so just plan on having fun with your grandchildren. This comment really troubled me, and I strongly disagreed with them at the time. They were dead wrong. I was able to maintain my relationship with my family and, at the same time, have a rewarding career. At one time, our department had a program where if you did not take a sick or personal day for a year, you would receive a certificate and partake in a small recognition ceremony. I had two options:

1. If I didn't use a family sick day at the end of the year, I could attend a ceremony, get a pin, and have my name written in a pamphlet.
2. The other option was to take three days off to witness the birth of my children and then help out at home.

It didn't take much thought to realize I had enough little pins and I also knew how my name looked on a piece of paper, so I always chose the latter. I am not encouraging the abuse of time off, but if you have earned time-off available, prioritize your life and use it. There is dedication to the job, but you can be too dedicated. If police officers fail to balance their priorities, in the long run, they will burn out and become ineffective in all areas of life.

Balance is the key to life, and police work is no exception. I assure you if you are or become a police officer, you will always be on the job. It takes discipline to create this balance, and you will need to do that.

The ceremony on my promotion to captain, with my family and friends (2002)

# PRO BONO PUBLICO

W hat is your department's mission statement? I am sure there is a full paragraph or page somewhere describing the mission of the department, but what does your shield or patch state? Remember, police officers wear shields, firemen wear badges. Our logo was "Pro Bono Publico." This will be your first lesson in Latin. Latin might be a dead language, but it still is present in many aspects of our modern language. Anyone in the medical profession can attest to this. "Pro Bono Publico" is Latin, meaning "For the public good." This was the motto on the uniform that I proudly wore for twenty-four years. It is a motto that sums up the role of a police officer in just three words. It is just as applicable today as it was to those enforcing laws decades and centuries ago.

Each law enforcement agency has a similar logo, some better than others. One of the most interesting ones I ever saw in my career was "We'll Try." Now that's not what I would call an encouraging mission statement. They didn't even try and hide it by using Latin. The department that sported this great phrase, thankfully, had since changed it because it certainly was not an accurate representation of the fine men and women who work there.

What are your officers wearing on their uniform? Is it something that they should be proud of? Is it a worthy goal they will strive for, or is it some stupid saying that has no relevance to their profession? This might seem like a trivial matter but something worth addressing.

What is the written mission statement of your department? This is the one that every officer reads during their induction and what every citizen expects from their police department. As we head into the twenty-first century, the mission statement can get quite muddied, so make sure your mission statement and the uniform is honoring to those men and women serving you as law enforcement officers.

The shoulder patch of the East Providence Police Department

# CHAPTER
# 5

# COMMUNITY-ORIENTED POLICING

One philosophy that I believe is muddying the mission of law enforcement today is that phrase I have hated since I first heard it. It nauseates me when I hear it being propagandized—"community-oriented policing." This is a NEW philosophy that started in the late 1980s and built up steam in the 1990s. If it follows the trend of other vogue policing techniques, it will eventually fade away. Now the true principles in "community policing" are basic policing principles. You could find a book on police work published in the 1800s, and a lot of the NEW community policing principles would be there. During my whole career, there has always been the vogue crime, and community policing was definitely vogue during the 1990s, yet I think it has been the most destructive to the mission of police work in recent history.

I will not go into great detail about community policing as there are more than enough books available that describe it ad nauseam. Basically, it involves that officers will be assigned specific regional areas that they are responsible for and then are given the authority to solve problems in that area, which will prevent crime, without the need to go through an extensive chain of command. It also encourages them to use problem-solving policing. Problem-solving policing? Now what would the opposite of that be? Non–problem-solving policing. Of course, police officers solve problems! That is why they were hired, and that is why communities have police departments—to solve problems. This is another one of those areas where someone takes the obvious and makes a whole new concept out of it, and yes, it costs a lot of money to develop and institute this concept. Why did community-oriented policing become a thing? I believe it is because academia and the social scientists had instituted so many other ridiculous policing theories and practices in the earlier part of the twentieth century that gutted basic policing so badly that they had to do something to stem the increase of crime. The Kansas City, Missouri, study back in the 1970s is just one of those studies that comes to mind, but there are many.

Community policing is also a part of that current trend to change words and meanings. You know we don't have secretaries and garbage men anymore; we now have office managers and ecology departments. The latter is actually used. We no longer have suspects but "persons of interest" and "actors." The biggest meaning change focused in community policing is "quality-of-life issues." Quality-of-life issues are supposed to be the problems that a local community sees as the problem they want the police force to focus on. It is amazing what the community sees as a quality-of-life issue. The trouble is that so much attention gets focused on these quality-of-life issues—such as too many unneutered cats in the neighborhood, not enough swings for all the children at the playground— that everyone forgets about the basic quality-of-life issues. I think most people are very concerned about basic quality-of-life issues and assume that their police department makes them a priority as well. Such basic quality-of-life issues I believe most people are concerned with and might express are the following:

- "I don't want to be murdered, kidnapped, raped, or robbed."
- "I don't want my family members to be murdered, kidnapped, raped, or robbed."
- "I also don't want someone burglarizing my home or stealing my car because all these things will really affect the quality of my life."

This is where departments and officers need to stay focused on police matters and keep the fluff to a minimum. This can easily be done by informing your community just what you are doing. Citizens want to know if their community is safe and, if not, what steps the police department is taking to make it safe.

Now I am not going to throw the baby out with the bathwater as community policing has some very good concepts and basic policing that should be implemented. I, however, relate it to someone reinventing the wheel, calling it a circular disk, and then encouraging everyone else to call it the circular disk. When you don't call it the circular disk but insist on calling it a wheel, you are old-fashioned and out of touch. Community policing has generated a lot of hype, millions of dollars in grants, and in my opinion, caused a lot of damage to the profession.

Now "community-oriented, problem-solving policing" sounds good, but this is really what policing has been from the beginning. It is simple. The community wants to be crime free and have order maintained. They ask their elected officials to establish a police force. The government establishes a police force and delegates them to stop crime and maintain order. This was identified back in the early 1800s by Sir Robert Peel who founded one of the first police departments, the Metropolitan Police in England.

The following is from Wikipedia (2018) with the Old English left in:

> The Peelian principles summarize the ideas that Sir Robert Peel developed to define an ethical police force. The approach expressed in these principles is commonly known as policing by consent in the United Kingdom and other countries such as Canada, Australia and New Zealand.
>
> In this model of policing, police officers are regarded as citizens in uniform. They exercise their powers to police their fellow citizens with the implicit consent of those fellow citizens. "Policing by consent" indicates that the legitimacy of policing in the eyes of the public is based upon a general consensus of support that follows from transparency about their powers, their integrity in exercising those powers and their accountability for doing so.
>
> The nine Peelian principles were as follows:
>
> 1. To prevent crime and disorder as an alternative to their repression by military force and severity of legal punishment.
> 2. To recognise always that the power of the police to fulfil their functions and duties is dependent on public approval of their existence, actions and behaviour, and on their ability to secure and maintain public respect.

3. To recognise always that to secure and maintain the respect and approval of the public means also the securing of the willing cooperation of the public in the task of securing observance of laws.

4. To recognise always that the extent to which the cooperation of the public can be secured diminishes proportionately the necessity of the use of physical force and compulsion for achieving police objectives.

5. To seek and preserve public favour, not by pandering to public opinion, but by constantly demonstrating absolutely impartial service to law, in complete independence of policy, and without regard to the justice or injustice of the substance of individual laws, by ready offering of individual service and friendship to all members of the public without regard to their wealth or social standing, by ready exercise of courtesy and friendly good humour, and by ready offering of individual sacrifice in protecting and preserving life.

6. To use physical force only when the exercise of persuasion, advice and warning is found to be insufficient to obtain public cooperation to an extent necessary to secure observance of law or to restore order, and to use only the minimum degree of physical force which is necessary on any particular occasion for achieving a police objective.

7. To maintain at all times a relationship with the public that gives reality to the historic tradition that the police are the public and that the public are the police, the police being only members of the public who are paid to give full-time attention to duties which are incumbent on every citizen in the interests of community welfare and existence.

8. To recognise always the need for strict adherence to police-executive functions, and to refrain from even seeming to usurp the powers of the judiciary, of avenging individuals or the State, and of authoritatively judging guilt and punishing the guilty.

9. To recognise always that the test of police efficiency is the absence of crime and disorder, and not the visible evidence of police action in dealing with them.

When I started the job in 1979, the East Providence Police Department practiced community-oriented, problem-solving policing. We just didn't call it community-oriented, problem-solving policing;

we just called it police work. The department's philosophy in 1979 was this. Officers were assigned to a specific geographic location: posts (also known as districts, beats, sector, etc., in other departments) and a specific shift for a year. At the end of the year, officers had the option of switching assignments, but for the year, they were responsible for what was happening on their post. There were relief officers to fill in vacancies, but even those officers would tend to work in a specific geographic area. The department had established a system to allow officers to investigate crimes and then follow them up. The department had established two substations on the two ends of a twelve-mile-long city to provide access for citizens and allow officers to remain in their assigned area. Officers were held accountable for crime patterns on their post. We were held accountable not only by supervisors but also by our fellow officers. A trip to the captain's office for messing up was a lot easier than winning the "gold brick award" or the "cry baby award" at the monthly union meeting. If you "won," you would actually be presented with a brick, spray-painted gold, or a pacifier at the meeting. Yes, it was in front of all the officers in attendance. Yes, you better have had the courage to walk up and receive your reward as well. These were obviously not coveted awards. Although you will not find it in many and nowadays any management books, peer pressure sure works, and police unions, in fact, hold their members accountable.

In the early 1980s, Capt. Richard Ferreira's vision was instrumental in having our records computerized. We could track crime patterns, suspect data, and even have a crude way of identifying suspects from a fingerprint left at a crime scene through a computer. This was long before the automated fingerprint identification system (AFIS) came along. There were many other policies and procedures in place that mimicked the current community-policing model long before the term was coined.

Community policing can cause confusion in the department's mission. I know as I was a victim of this scourge when our own mission statement was reviewed in the late nineties. Several of us sat and reviewed the mission statement as it was proposed. The draft read as follows:

> **The mission of the East Providence Police Department is to create and maintain a proactive partnership with our residential and business community in an effort to enhance public safety and reduce the fear of crime within the City of East Providence.**

Something was bothering me about what we reviewed, but I couldn't put a finger on it. My partner at the time, Lt. Steve Enos, also a like-minded thinker about community policing, was also having trouble with it. It was not until the next day when he reviewed it with me that he pointed out that we had forgotten a very important element. The final version then read as follows:

> **The mission of the East Providence Police Department is to** *protect life, property, and civil order while creating and maintaining* **a proactive partnership with our residential and business community in an effort to enhance public safety and reduce the fear of crime within the City of East Providence.**

We had all forgotten to include the part about preserving life, property, and public order—the public good. We had all our community partnerships covered, but our basic task was missing. Now this was not a major issue and was easily corrected, but it was just an example of how thinking can be redirected.

The one theme that community policing propaganda professes, which I believe to be correct, is that it needs to be a department-wide philosophy, not an individualized unit. This, however, is the one area that often seems to be most overlooked. For police departments to buy into the fact that community policing is the best invention since sliced bread, then why would they not implement it wholeheartedly? Time and time again, administrations feel that community policing on a department level will not work. Therefore, they try to gradually integrate it into the department by creating the "community-policing unit." If everyone working on any team is not on the same page, there will be problems, and policing is no exception. This division unintentionally creates the "A" team and the "B" team within the department. The new "A" team is usually outfitted in a new uniform, which is often the equivalent of Power Ranger's pajamas, and then they are released to solve all the woes of the city. Those officers not on the "A" team start to feel out of the loop, and moral and productivity starts to decline among them. Meanwhile, the "A" team soon realizes they aren't faster than a speeding locomotive; they can't stop bullets, jump tall buildings in a single bound, or solve all the policing problems on their own. The outcome is burnout in the "A" team, and you now have both teams working below their potential, not completing the mission. In the end, when the community-policing grants run out, municipalities often fail to supplement these positions, and it is back to square one.

Your department's mission statement needs to be clear, realistic, time-proven, inclusive, and achievable. It is great to try new ideas and technologies, but the mission needs to stay on a firm foundation, and the entire department needs to be on board.

The greatest example of community policing I ever saw existed in one of our districts, Riverside, Rhode Island. Now it is actually a unique geographic area within the city of East Providence, but the residents were so comfortable with the officers assigned there that they would ask for a "Riverside" officer to speak to if they were unfamiliar with the officer sent. Capt. Joe Crevier, Sgt. Walter Cook, Lt. James Trail, Cpl. Stephen Crowley (my field training officer), Cpl. Bob Souza, Cpl. Frank Hurley, Cpl. Joseph Ford, Cpl. John Ciallela, Cpl. Walter Muzzy, Cpl. Gordon Remond, Cpl. Ernest DiRocco, and Cpl. Peter DeAquiar made up the "Riverside Police Department."

They knew almost everyone, and almost everyone knew them. This may sound unbelievable to those unfamiliar with the situation, but for those of us who worked during this era, it is a known fact. The crime rate in this area was minimal and were mostly misdemeanors. When a series of serious crimes emerged, most often it was quickly solved with the dedication of these officers and the wonderful support of the citizens of Riverside. These officers didn't go to school to become community police officers. They were exceptional police officers who lived in this community and wanted to be a part of maintaining it. The residents respected this dedication. Aside from an egged windshield or a little spray paint, these officers were off-limits. Violations of that unwritten code were maintained within the criminal element who lived there. At the end of the shift, you might join one of these officers at the local bar, and sitting next to you were some of the people you recently arrested. Nothing was said. It was truly a unique experience. Actually, on a few occasions, one of these individuals bought me a beer and told me that they deserved to be arrested for such and such. We would often make jokes about this, but the reality was if your municipality could replicate what they did, you would have a much better municipality.

I was assigned to work in Riverside for two years but never had the connection that the named above officers did. The one thing I knew, especially working in this area, was that respect was crucial. Regardless of the person's record, as I have mentioned earlier in this book, it was imperative to start with respect if the situation allowed. (When two guys are beating each other to a pulp, not an uncommon site in Riverside, you don't need to worry about your opening remark.) The other uniqueness about this area was that it was geographically a long way away from help. For the most part, there were two officers assigned to this area, and you knew the closest help was about ten minutes away on a good traffic day. My most memorable moment regarding this was at three in the morning, the other officer assigned to Riverside was tied up with an arrest in the center of the city. I located three individuals walking through a neighborhood who appeared to be out of place. Rhode Island had, maybe still does, a law dealing with being "abroad in the night," so I stopped them to see what they were doing. One I recognized as a local biker, the other two I did not. I remember that two of the three were much larger than me and the third looked wired up. I approached them.

"Good evening, gentlemen. Could I see some ID?" I asked.

Immediately, the wired-up one started getting defensive, but within seconds, the biker slapped him on the back of the head and grabbed him.

"He's doing his job, and he asked you politely. Show him your ID."

All three complied, and after a brief warrants check, we conversed, and they were on their way. I too was on my way, breathing a sigh of relief.

A few months later, this biker approached me one day and thanked me for having the balls to confront them and acting like a gentleman. Months later, this same individual was locked up by another officer. When I saw him in the cell block, he asked for a smoke. Now obviously, this is against policy, but this is one of those times you use some common sense. I took him out, gave him a cigar to smoke, and brought him back into the cell.

A few years later, I was with my family at Rocky Point Amusement Park. Unknown to me, they were having a rock concert that night. I saw the crowd quickly changing from families to a hard rock crowd setting up. Now the security for the band was a local bike gang. All of a sudden, I heard my name yelled out very loudly from the band area. I looked up and saw this same individual. He walked over with several of his associates. He walked up, shook my hand, and proceeded to tell his associates what a great cop I was. Again, a moment of relief. I don't relay this to pat myself on the back as I actually did nothing out of the ordinary and actually, at one point, violated department policy by letting him have a smoke. I relay it to show that respect and a little common sense go a long way in being a good ambassador for your police department and personally make your job a lot easier and safer.

Another situation regarding respect that came up related to another individual who would have contact with us almost on a weekly basis. His arrests started when he was a juvenile and continued throughout his progression into organized crime. I and other officers arrested him dozens of times and not always without resistance. I would not call our relationship cordial; however, one day, after making the rank of sergeant, he approached me. He did not complain about his arrests or how he was treated but asked, "You never disrespected me. Officer such and such arrested me the other day, and he was very disrespectful to me and my fiancée who was there. I deserved it, she did not. Could you please speak to him about showing her respect in the future?"

Here was an individual who was very capable of putting a bullet in your head, yet he was asking for something very basic. Yes, I spoke to the officer, and the problem was resolved. Common sense and respect go a long way. You need to use both whenever possible.

So what is the future of community policing, and how should you deal with it? If your department has a fragmented department with a separate community policing unit, you are going to have to deal with it. You might be one of those exceptions where it ends up working. If not, give it time; either it will implode, or the department will eventually institute community-policing principles department-wide, which is a good thing if they keep the basic law enforcement mission and avoid a lot of the fluff. Regardless of your department's structure and where you are assigned, be a good police officer and do your job. Remember, the people of your community need you to be the best police officer you can be for them. If you want to get more involved in your community, then by all means do so. Coach a youth sports team. Become a mentor for some child. Participate in a local community group. There are many ways you can make an impact on your community if you care. And if you care, do it on your own time. Show that you really want to make an impact in your community. Your shift should not be to be assigned as a coach on the soccer field while your coworkers are out dodging bullets.

If you are an administrator, please read the paragraphs above.

If you are a citizen, observe. Look at the crime rate in your community. Do you feel safe going out in your community? Do you feel safe going out at night? Do you feel safe going into every neighborhood of your community at night? Do you constantly worry whether your car will be where you parked it in the morning? Or will it only be the shell of your car? It is not only "Do you feel safe?" but also "Are you safe?" I don't care how many block parties your police department sponsors; the proof of how successful your police department is found in how safe you feel and how safe you are in your community. If you don't feel safe or the statistics show that you are not safe, encourage your elected officials to look at taking a new philosophy so that you will be safe in your community and have a positive "quality of life" experience.

CHAPTER

6

# PATROL OPERATIONS
# THE CORNERSTONE OF POLICING

P atrol operations is where every officer should start and further spend
a few years before any promotion. Anyone who works in the law
enforcement profession who has not spent some time on the street as a
patrol officer is lacking this basic building block of policing. I know that
there are many people in the law enforcement profession who never spent
any time working in patrol. Many analysts, chiefs, colonels, commissioners,
and advisors working in law enforcement throughout the country today
have unfortunately never worked as a patrol officer. I am not going to
judge their performance; only you can do that. I wouldn't be surprised
to learn that someone who never worked patrol started the community
policing trend. Regardless of how they are doing, they have missed
something that, I believe, is very important. On a side note to this, the
once a month or once a year "I'm going to go out on patrol today" as the
local-media cameras flash does not count for real patrol work. For those in
a command situation who never worked in patrol, I suggest that you work
some night shifts between eight in the evening and four in the morning,
just to get a feel of what your officers are actually experiencing. How is
the communication equipment actually working? Are there enough people
assigned to handle the calls? Is there enough room in the cruiser for the
officer to be comfortable after all the gadgets are installed? (This includes
the officers who are over six-ft tall as well.) Are officers able to stay out in
the street while they do their reports? How long does an arrest take based
on the policies you have instituted?

I am not going to get into specifics about patrol operations as they are going to be specific to each region and community, but I am going to provide an overview on how to make patrol fun, easy, and productive. Your first job as a patrol officer is to be a good investigator—yes, an investigator. Just like a detective working a homicide, you should be looking to solve crimes, not merely report them. Monkeys could be trained to go out and take crime reports. We need police officers to take crime reports and then investigate them, with the goal of solving the crime. You need to ask the famous "who, what, where, when, why, and how" questions. Not only do you need to ask those questions, but you also need to get the answers. As a patrolman, this fact was drilled into us by my first line supervisor Sgt. Bill Sloyer, the guy I got to call Billy now. His famous line was "Remember, you're not report takers. You're investigators."

Although he coined the phrase for me, there were a few supervisors I worked for who expected anything less. Your department should expect nothing less either.

A questions you might hear in response to this is "How can I patrol and be an investigator?"

If this is a tough question for you, you might be one of those you should consider a new career.

"I'm too busy, flat out."

Maybe you're too busy because you don't take the time to solve problems or INVESTIGATE.

A police department's approach to patrol operations will greatly affect the overall performance of the department. Are your patrol officers used for police work, or are they used to run errands and act as chauffeurs? When I first got on the job, one of my first duties at the start of the shift was to run to the local coffee shop and pick up the free coffees for the officer in charge. It was not a big deal to get the lieutenant a coffee, but I found that the officer in charge had attracted a herd of civilian ticks who just happened to come into the police station to hang around at four o'clock every afternoon. The coffee run would end up being two trays worth of coffee along with a variety of other items. After a few months of this, along with dealing with the dumbfounded look I got every time from the clerks who were probably making minimum wage at the coffee shop, I got tired of it. I told the manager to start charging me for the order, which he did. When I brought in the first receipt and told the group the total, the looks on their faces were priceless. Needless to say, the herd moved on, and I didn't get stuck with this job anymore. Not long after this, Lieutenant

Lynch, doing some proactive patrol, decided to make a gambling raid at a local bar. About twenty people were arrested, including the manager of this donut shop. As the manager watched, sitting in handcuffs, while the arresting officers consumed endless cups of free coffee and donuts from his shop, he decided to finally end the coffee welfare program.

Are your patrol officers encouraged to enforce laws, solve problems, and catch criminals? Or are they encouraged not to rock the boat and, when a problem arises, just to go out make a good presence? For those of you who think the criminal element runs away when they see you drive up in your marked car, looking big and bad, I have news for you. They catch on quick. They realize that you are not serious about solving the problem and that you have to leave sooner or later. Once you leave, they can go back to creating your problem. The criminal element needs to know you are determined to solve problems, including the ones they are creating.

I had the pleasure to have Sgt. John Andrews working with me many nights during my time in the patrol division, and I thank him for being by my side as we solved these problems. As for conducting investigations, I was also fortunate to have some great mentors, especially Sgt. George Thomas, Lt. Stephen Crowshaw, and Lt. John Lynch. They were excellent at teaching new officers the investigative techniques needed to go beyond taking the initial police report and actually work on solving the crime.

Regardless of your department's policy on patrol operations, what is your policy? How do you look at patrol officers, or if you are one, what do you perceive your job to be? Do you see yourself as the backbone of the police department? Do you see yourself as the person who will be making the first impression—the ambassador of your department—with the average citizens? These are important questions you must ask yourself. When working in patrol, you are, in fact, the backbone of the department. You are on the frontline, preserving life, property, and public order. You are probably going to be the first law enforcement officer most people interact with, and their impression of the law enforcement profession is going to be influenced by you.

If you don't perceive yourself as being the most vital link in a law enforcement agency, then I would encourage you to do some soul-searching as I believe you will come to the same conclusion I did. You, the patrol officer, are the backbone of your police department.

Early 1980s with the "Paddy Wagon"

# CHAPTER 7

## PATROL OPERATIONS

## POLICE REPORTS AND THE RED PEN

Documenting what you do as a police officer is imperative. Once you are hired, police reports are now going to be a major part of your life. You can be an excellent police officer and do everything right, but if you don't properly document it, all your work is for naught. Police reports will follow you throughout your career, regardless of what division you are assigned to, but I put them under patrol as that is where you will start writing them.

*The "red pen."* Since retiring, whenever I run into officers who worked for me when I was a supervisor, the red pen is almost always mentioned. The reason for this is that as a supervisor, part of my job was to review officers' reports. In the era of paper reports, I would always correct them with a red pen. When we went to computerized reports, upon completion, they would print out the report, and I would correct them with a red pen. Although it is a point of humor now, not one officer regrets this aspect of their career. We all became better officers through correction, and I certainly had many periods of my career where I was on the other end of the "red pen."

I not only corrected grammatical errors in reports but also corrected reports so that officers could present their report to someone unfamiliar with the circumstances who, after reading the report, would have a clear picture of who was involved, what happened, when it happened, where it happened, how it happened, and hopefully, why it happened. In criminal cases involving an arrest, it is important to include the elements of the crime, not just assume them, based on the title of the offense. It was further important for them to document the investigative actions they followed to ensure that case would not be thrown out on a technicality because it was not documented. As the corrector, I was not the most popular person, and I am sure considered a "pain in the ——" by many. As we transitioned into word processors, officers could easily update portions of their reports, and this angst diminished a bit. When it was paper only, we used cases of Wite-Out, and the newest gadget for this was quickly adopted. It was a nuisance and not good for popularity votes, but in the end, it was for the benefit of all. I was not quite as harsh as a counterpart who would simply have the officers pull up to below the shift commander's window (the office was on the second floor) and toss the report out while quietly saying, "Do it over." You may think that this technique, especially the latter, is harsh. It is not. Officers are making life-and-death decisions, and they need to protect not only the citizens but also the department and themselves as well. A poor police report with a lack of documented facts can lead to criminals being released, departments getting sued, and officers getting disciplined. It is much easier to pick up a report from the ground, or one covered in red ink, and do it over than it is to sit in a witness box in court, being grilled by a defense attorney about what is lacking in your report. The focus of the questions will be implying that if you are too stupid to correctly write a report, how can the rest of your actions be accurate and believable? "Red pens" are private. A public testimony is a part of the public record.

Police reports first document what you are doing. As a public servant, the citizens have a right to know why they are paying for a police department. A report is one mean by which you can justify, not only the number of officers you currently have budgeted within your department but also maybe the need to increase the size of your police department.

You as a police officer want to be rightly paid a decent salary. Let your reports reflect that fact by demonstrating through writing that you are a very intelligent professional person who is making a difference in the community where you are employed. After writing your report, proofread it. Does the narrative sound as if a professional wrote it, or does it sound like something you might find in a fourth-grade English class? Cops can be their own worst enemies sometimes, and this is one of the areas in which they do it often.

Who, what, where, why, when and how—these should all be included in your report. If definite answers cannot be provided, then you need to document what information is available to you at the time so these answers can be eventually found. When investigating a crime, the victim and witnesses may not know the name of the suspect. "Unknown suspect" may be a correct entry when the suspect is unknown, but it is not a correct entry for an investigator. Be an investigator and ask some follow-up questions. After you are done, it may still be an "unknown suspect," but you now have identifying information that will narrow the scope of your search down. It could be an unknown suspect who is described as being a white male, approximately six-foot tall, heavy built, with brown hair, trimmed goatee, and a tattoo of a heart on his right bicep. He was wearing a brown T-shirt, blue jeans ripped at the bottom, and brown work boots. He had a pack of Marlboro cigarettes sticking out of his back pocket.

Document all the details and be so descriptive so that the reader who has no knowledge of the incident can feel as if they were there. Most police departments will have mandatory fields, requesting descriptions of the people, places, and items involved. Don't allow your report to end with the "required fields." Don't do the bare minimum; excel as an investigator. For example, if the questions relate to a suspect's vehicle, expand beyond the required data—year, make, model, color, and VIN number. Describe anything that is unique to the vehicle in question. This could include a multitude of items that are not part of the "required fields." Is there body damage? What is the location of the damage? Is there a unique paint scheme? Are there bumper stickers? Where, how many, and what do they say? Are there any aftermarket accessories on the vehicle?

I realize the more you describe, the more time it is going to take you to complete your report. You may consider leaving out the "inconsequential facts" to allow you to more quickly complete the report, but always consider what the long-term effects of doing that are. What time you save now condensing your report may lend itself to spending a lot of time in the chief's office later, explaining why something was not done or, worse, spending time as a defendant in a civil case accused of failing to act properly.

When writing a police report, you need to combine good grammar with technical writing. You are not writing and incorporating proper synonyms and style to be graded on your essay or creative writing skills as you would in a college writing course. You are writing to be clear and concise so you can document your investigation. Don't worry about being repetitive as you proceed. Pronouns have a place in essay writing but not in police reports. There should be no doubt about whom or what you are referring to when writing your police report. Include the victim's, witness's, or suspect's name in each sentence. It will sound robotic, but it will help eliminate any possible confusion for a defense attorney to banter about in front of a jury at a later date.

Your police report should be inclusive and in chronological order. It should include all facts relating to the case and your investigation. Your report should be based on the assumption that someone will be able to pick up a report, read it, and continue the investigation from the point where you left off. If there are leads you wanted to follow but could not, explain the circumstances on why you didn't. If the evidence observed is in conflict to what the victim is saying to you, you need to document these facts. Your police report should be based on facts. They should not be based on your opinion. Police investigations are to determine the truth, not to support a preconceived opinion of what you think happened. Your job as a police officer is to determine the truth, and this is partly accomplished with a well-written police report. At the end of your investigation, your fact-based report will be sufficient in documenting the "probable cause" that existed for you to make an arrest. In court, your report will establish the "beyond a reasonable doubt" that is needed for a criminal conviction.

Just as your report will support your decision to make an arrest, it will also support your decision not to make an arrest. If a case needs further investigation or misses elements of a crime or lacks probable cause, conclude your report with the facts that lead you to that conclusion. If, after your investigation, you feel that there is no crime, document why you came to this conclusion.

There will be a variety of reports you are required to prepare based on the needs and guidelines of your department. Basically, there will be a uniformed crime report. This will be the one with the standardized fields where you are documenting the basics of the incident. The data used from these reports is often the information used to build databases, allowing you to target crime and provide crime statistics not only for your agency but also for the databases maintained on a state and national level. The FBI uniformed crime report gets its data based on what your agency reports to them.

Statements are those reports taken from victims, witnesses, and defendants. Although all reports are part of the permanent record, these reports reflect actual statements. They are then signed and witnessed by another individual. When taking a statement from an individual, it should be recorded verbatim. Don't put words in their mouth. If an individual has a basic vocabulary and the signed statement has words within it from your "a new word every day" calendar, you and your witness may have to explain this language in a court of law. Whenever taking a signed statement, make sure to include the printed name of the witness along with the date, time, and location of the statement along with the name of the officer taking the statement and a witness, often another officer working on the case. One technique that is helpful, if allowed by your department, is to have the individual write out the statement. It may not be as neat and legible as a typed statement, but its authenticity is much harder to challenge. This is also a good tool when you are shorthanded and have multiple statements to take for a case. As with all investigations, keep your witnesses separated when possible. You don't want a compilation of what everybody agrees upon; you want their individual statement. By having them write out their own statements, it not only keeps the individuals separated but also allows the data to be gathered in an efficient manner. After a statement is completed and corrections are needed to be made, make sure both you and the person making the corrections initial the corrections. This is also a good tool for demonstrating that a person actually reviewed their statement.

After concluding your report, it needs to be reviewed by a supervisor who will make a final recommendation. Maybe they will agree with your conclusion, or maybe they will point you in a different direction or refer it to another division. If you are a high-ranking officer, have the officer directly below you review it. Although you are unlikely to be investigating street crimes at this level, you are very likely going to be doing internal investigations, and it is important to get a second opinion before making your report a part of the permanent record.

As I talk about in another chapter, there needs to be a standardized policy on where the report goes after preparing it. I know we live in the "paperless age," but I strongly recommend printing out hard copies. These hard copies need to have a place to be forwarded to and stored in an orderly manner. If you are truly working in a digital environment where paper does not exist, there needs to be a system in place where this report can be tracked and accessed in a timely manner.

There are many courses, seminars, and books available for writing police reports, and if you are a part of this profession, I encourage you to expand your ability to write an excellent police report. Police reports are one of the least liked tasks police officers will have to perform, but they are certainly one of the most important tasks police officers will be required to do. A good police report will have a lasting impact on your overall goal of solving and preventing crime.

# PATROL OPERATIONS
# THE DEPARTMENT'S AMBASSADOR

Cpl. Bob Pacheco once told me you only get one chance to make a first impression. When you first encounter someone, there are going to be many variables people see in you: size, age, sex, color, etc., all which are out of your control. The first thing you can control is your appearance. You are a uniformed patrol officer, and you should look sharp—a basic policy. If you come across as someone who has it together, you will be afforded that respect. Even criminals are sizing you up. Don't think for a moment that your appearance does not affect how they will interact with you and influence what they will try to get away with, including physical harm against you.

The uniform should provide comfort to the officer while projecting authority. It should readily recognize the officer's department, rank, and badge number. It should have the department's shoulder patch. I realize there are individual differences, and provisions must be in place so that a shift can rapidly adjust to the present weather conditions, and a balance needs to be drawn between appearance and functionality. I mention this as there are departments that set dates for short- or long-sleeve shirts among other things. If you ever lived in New England, you realize this just does not work. Your day shift will be in short sleeves, while the officers at midnight are wearing leather jackets. In short, there needs to be a uniform policy that provides for overall uniformity while considering practicality.

*Merriam-Webster's Dictionary* defines "uniform" as follows:

> A dress of distinctive design or fashion worn by members of
> a particular group and serving as a means of identification;
> broadly: distinctive or characteristic clothing.

Uniform hats are another issue. I strongly believe that officers should wear a uniform hat whenever they are out of the car, interacting with the public, providing crowd control or traffic control. They serve as a means of identification and project a professional appearance. That being said, uniform police hats are basically uncomfortable. They should not be worn when not necessary. There are some departments that require officers to wear their hats while driving in a marked police cruiser. I think this is taking a good appearance a bit too far. They look sharp and serve a purpose out in the public, but to require officers to wear hats while they drive a car, in my opinion, is not serving any purpose. I really think that if an individual cannot identify the car as a police car based on its markings, lights, and uniformed driver, then whether or not the hat is on the head of the officer is a moot point.

You will find that community policing has introduced a whole new line of uniforms to policing. On one end of the spectrum is the pajama crowd—the polo shirt, casual pants, sneakers, baseball cap, and usually, some ridiculous braided necklace around their neck, promoting the latest good cause. So lax is this uniform that you might have a hard time picking out the cop in a lineup with five other civilians in casual dress. This is the uniform designed not to be intimidating or scary. Instead of a nice, shiny shield, they usually have a cute little logo embroidered on the shirt. Visible guns tend to be optional too because they can be scary. It makes an officer look very relaxed. The last thing you want a criminal to perceive in you is that you are relaxed.

On the other end of this spectrum is the officers in full battle gear. You will usually find these uniforms coming out about a year after the "A" team has been in place. Community policing has worked so well that there are areas of the city that are no longer manageable. Even the police cannot go into some of these areas. In response, the tactical uniform has been developed. This is the getup that most third-world countries' armies envy. There is no lack of an intimidating look or weapons on this setup. This definitely does not send the kinder and gentler message. Now every department should have a tactical unit that dresses for full combat when tactical situations arise but not the officer on the beat. If everyday policing in your jurisdiction is a tactical situation, then you need to get back to the basics.

I had an experience with the latter. I was attending a comic-con in a large city. If you are not familiar with comic-cons, I recommend you do an Internet search. I observed three men dressed in combat gear. I sincerely thought they were attached to the *Ghostbusters* group dressed in costume until I got close and saw they were actually police officers on duty. I really think that if something happened requiring them to take action, the crowd, at first, would have assumed they were part of the show, role playing.

The second area of your first impression that you can control is your mouth. Remember the principle—God gave you two ears and ONE mouth. That means you should listen twice as much as you talk. When you talk, you should be polite, professional, and sound as if you knew what you were talking about. Every encounter with an individual who is not posing an immediate threat should start this way. The individual can set the tone for subsequent dialogue, but your initial utterance should be the same for everyone. Remember the golden rule: "Do unto others as you would have done unto you."

How would you expect someone in authority to interact with your wife, husband, daughter, son, mother, or father? Remember, when you interact with someone as a police officer, you are an authority figure, and you are speaking to someone's wife, husband, daughter, son, mother, or father.

Now that you know how you should look and act, what should you actually do? Every department should have specific duties and responsibilities of a patrol officer written out. Depending on the region and the department, there will be variations, but basically, it is to carry out the mission of the department—protect life, property, and preserve order. You first do this by getting out of the police station and into the community. Lt. Commander V. Geberth of the N.YPD once identified a small group of police officers as the type "Who wants to hang around headquarters dressed up like dogs."

Does the name *McGruff* ring any bells? Hopefully, this is not what you signed up for. The "dog" job should be reserved for the sick, lame, and lazy. The community needs you on the street. Your brother and sister officers need you on the street.

# PATROL OPERATIONS

# TECHNIQUES OF PATROL

*P*atrolman, *patrolwoman*, and *patrol officer* all have the word *patrol* within it. Patrolling is a basic function of any law enforcement agency. Just what do I mean by *patrol operations*? *Webster's Dictionary's definition* of *PATROL* is

> n. (1664) a: the action of traversing a district or beat or of going the rounds along a chain of guards for observation or the maintenance of security. b. the person performing such an action. c. a unit of persons or vehicles employed for reconnaissance, security, or combat.

*Webster's Dictionary's* definition of *PATROLMAN* is

> n. (1867) one who patrols, especially a policeman assigned to a beat.

If you take note of the dates above, you will see that the function of patrolling has been around for centuries. Our rules defined the job of a patrol officer as existing in order to provide for the primary law enforcement and public safety functions within the police department. Patrol operations in a law enforcement agency can be both proactive and reactive. Proactive patrol is encouraging officers to go out and find and act upon potential criminal activity. Reactive patrol is simply having officers respond to calls for service from its citizens. A good police department should have a balance of both. Hopefully, if your department is doing enough proactive patrol, then the number of calls for service will decrease. What is your department's policy? Is there an unwritten rule for officers not to seek out problems? No crime discovered equals decreased crime rates that are great for statistics and politicians but not so great for the citizens if crime is really happening and not being reported and addressed. Increased crime rates accompanied by increased clearance rates are not a bad thing if the long-term projection of crime is steadily decreasing.

Reactive patrol is pretty straightforward. A citizen will contact the police department to report a situation. Or a citizen may just wave down a patrol officer and relay their issue. Once alerted, officers are assigned to investigate the incident. This should now be followed through in a prompt manner with your inquisitive mind in gear. Response times are very crucial. Not only does it mean the difference between life and death, but sometimes it is also again reflective of your ambassadorship. If for some reason there is going to be a delay in responding to a call for service, the caller needs to be made aware of this. If your response times are very high, this is not good. Our emergency calls had an average response time from time of call to the first officer arriving at the scene at less than one minute. For nonemergency calls, our average response time was less than ten minutes.

In my opinion, proactive patrol is the area that patrol officers should focus their energy on. The East Providence Police Department had and still has a great reputation for encouraging officers to proactively patrol. Proactive patrol is done in many ways. Once you are on the street, patrol; see the definition above. Whether you walk, drive a car, ride a bicycle, or ride a horse, get into the community you are assigned to and patrol it. You will soon become familiar with what is normal and be able to identify what is not normal, potential problems. The more familiar you become with an area, the easier it will be for you to identify things that are out of place. Remember, your job is to take care of small problems as well as large ones. Some officers have the idea that they are in a holding pattern until some mass murderer needs to be apprehended, and in the meantime, they cannot get tied up with little nuisances. This is one of those areas where I agree with community policing. Be proactive and take care of the small problems. By handling the small problems, not only are you going to reduce the larger problems, but also when the larger problem comes along, you will know what to do. You will know what to do because you have had the practice and experience dealing with the little things. If you develop your investigative techniques by solving minor thefts and assaults, you will be much better at solving robberies and homicides when you are confronted with them.

What are the little things? The list of petty, minor problems you will be called upon for are endless. The community policing gang calls these quality-of-life issues. Regardless of what they are called, you will encounter them daily. Of all the arrests and investigations done in my career, I received more documented thanks for the little things I resolved, including a ten-dollar tip.

It was two in the morning, and the lieutenant called me to go the elderly housing complex to meet with a woman about a strange noise. Upon investigating, the noise was found to be the stove fan that she did not know how to turn off. I could have just walked out and told her it was not a police problem. I could have told her to call the building superintendent. I could have forwarded the matter to elderly affairs. I opted to turn it off and showed her how to operate it. She immediately stuck a ten-dollar bill in my hand. I refused it, but she insisted. To simplify things, at two in the morning, I just left and put the money in her mailbox. Two days later, I received an envelope containing a ten-dollar bill along with a "thank you" note at the police station. If you just handle the little things, it makes life easier for all involved, and you act as a good ambassador for your police department.

Being proactive in identifying and correcting minor problems can go a long way in fulfilling your mission. Any potential hazard or unsafe condition on your beat should be reported as a means of protecting life and property. If you are patrolling your area and you notice the concrete on the bridge support is crumbling, report it; don't wait for it to collapse. By "report it" I mean document it in the official record somewhere. God forbid that if something happens, you know they will be looking for a scapegoat, and that path usually flows downhill. Remember the phrase "CYA." Redirect the flow back up. If there is a foot-deep pothole in the middle of the road, block it and get someone out to fix it. Don't wait for an accident. In the long run, the accident investigation will end up taking more of your time, and more importantly, you will possibly prevent someone from getting injured.

Preserving order is another area you can be proactive. What are the people in your assigned area doing? They should be going about their daily business, not impeded upon by others. Are there individuals or groups of individuals interfering with them? It is your job to identify this and correct it. Large groups of people chronically loitering in an area should be dealt with as a means of preserving order. First, determine what draws this crowd and if it is a problem. Is it a criminal activity or simply some lost souls with nothing better to do? Investigate, find the cause, and appropriately solve the problem.

Every department is going to have a particular problem that seems overwhelming. I once attended a community-policing seminar where one of the officers in attendance was very gloom and doom about this one area in his town where loitering had been a problem for generations and no solution seemed to be in sight. His question was "What type of community-policing action would help them in correcting this?" When some of our classmates felt he might be stretching the generational thing a bit, my coworker who was about fifty years old at this time piped in and said, "Yeah, I used to hang there all the time when I was a kid."

So in this scenario, the first question you have to ask is whether it is a problem. Knowing the area, I could see large groups of young people with their cars, meeting in front of numerous businesses, would be a distraction to customers. But what were the store managers actually saying about this congregation? In a similar scenario, in the next town over, there was a similar location known as Horgan's. That was the name of the drugstore in a plaza with numerous other stores, but the hangout was referred to as Horgan's. The unwritten rule was this: park your cars on the edge of the parking lot away from the all businesses, no visible alcohol, no drugs, and keep the noise down. This relationship went on for years until one day, someone decided to rob Horgan's in front of these "loiterers." The guy thought he would easily get away into the adjacent woods, never suspecting that the loiterers, who would subsequent to this night be called Horgan's heroes, would chase this guy down and bring him back for the police to arrest. This is a perfect example of how a police department knew how to foster relations and get the citizens involved in their community, long before "community policing" blazed its way into law enforcement.

Back to the original scenario, it involved not only loitering that the merchants were, in fact, complaining about but also illegal alcohol and drug use. The answer to this problem does not require a complex community-policing plan, but it requires persistence and innovation on the part of the police department, specifically the officers responsible for this area. The first step would be to start issuing warnings to encourage compliance because it had been going on for so long. Whoever did not understand this polite request would now be noticed when they committed the least motor-vehicle violation. Naturally, after you stopped these cars, you would look for evidence of illegal alcohol and drug use, which leads to probable cause, which leads to people and cars getting searched, which leads to cars being towed and people getting arrested. Eventually, the message gets out that this is not the cool place to be. This is problem-solving policing at its best. The main problem with a situation such as this is you and your department need to be committed to fixing the problem. The longer it has gone unchecked, the longer it may take to resolve.

I use this example as I am sure each city or town has a similar nuisance area. You need to determine if the nuisance is really a nuisance. If you or your supervisor determine it is a nuisance, you need to commit to solving the problem. If you read this and laughed because your particular problem involved nightly shootings not kids drinking, then it is time to apply the same principles. Camp out in the neighborhood. If it is that bad, put snipers on the roofs providing protection to your operation. Get the department of public works in there to clean the place out—the department of public works, not you. Become friendly with the local zoning officer and start condemning properties. After the city takes possession, have your fire department use them for training. Burn them to the ground. It gives the firefighters some great training and, at the same time, eliminates a nuisance in the community. Be creative and create a good quality of life for the many law-abiding citizens who are living there. Don't let the law-abiding citizens living anywhere in your community be terrorized daily.

When I first started on the job, I was soon working next to Lt. Steve Crowshaw on a nightly basis. Being five years as my senior, he was a great mentor and taught me many aspects of police work. One of these was how to deal with junk and abandoned cars on your post. Most cities have ordinances prohibiting junk and abandoned vehicles. We had one, but not much focus was placed on it during the in-house training. It seemed like such a trivial thing to me to place a tag on a car that then had to be removed in seven days. Lieutenant Crowshaw soon taught me the value of this tool with the peer pressure understanding that "my post" that was adjacent to "his post" was not going to become a junkyard. I soon realized that this is one of those little areas that can have a big impact on your community. Junk cars look terrible and have a negative impact on surrounding property values, and criminals also love them. They provide a means of storing and stashing contraband. Where junk cars are the norm, criminals know they can dump a wanted car, and it likely will not be quickly identified, allowing evidence to deteriorate. This is one of those "quality-of-life issues."

One time I will never forget regarding this is when I was working on a case that brought me into another jurisdiction, specifically in one of their high-crime areas. They had recently established a "community-policing" satellite police station in this same area. They had obviously spent time and money in refurbishing the building. In spite of this, I could not help but notice that within a six-block periphery of this station, there were enough junk cars to build a battleship. I believe their efforts would have been better spent doing something constructive rather than putting on a show. I am sure the majority of good, hardworking people who lived in this neighborhood would much rather see the place cleaned up and supplemented by regular patrols than have a substation built. Before saying anything, I asked Cpl. John Rossi who was riding with me at the time if he saw anything out of place. He immediately picked up on the same issue, identifying the perpetual junkyard covering the neighborhood. If you are going to have community policing, walk the walk; don't just talk the talk.

Another area that is essential to proactive patrol is the enforcement of traffic laws. These stops should not just focus on motor-vehicle violations but on what else is going on, hidden from site. Once you have established a probable cause to make the stop, you open up a whole new dynamic for yourself as an investigator. You can visually search a vehicle for contraband, and if additional probable cause is present, conduct a full search. Traffic stops are also a great way to determine if anyone is wanted. Maybe a crime was just committed by the occupants. Observe the condition of the occupants. Do they have blood on them? Are there clothes torn and filthy, possibly coming from breaking into a building? Short of reckless and impaired driving, your main focus should be on what else is going on with this vehicle and the occupants you have stopped.

Although I had hundreds of proactive arrests generated from car stops, there is a particular one that sticks out. Lt. Ralph Ezovski and I were returning from a prisoner transport from the city of Providence. As we were driving through Downtown Providence, we noticed a Providence cruiser stop a vehicle with three individuals in it. As is the unwritten rule, we stopped to back the officer up. Another Providence officer arrived shortly and told us the car was stopped for excessive speeding. After the stop, the officer relayed that one of the occupants had placed something under the seat. Because of this, they were taken out of the car and patted down. During the pat down, we found that each of the occupants had a lock knife in their possession. It was dark, so the knives were seized and secured on our persons while we each continued our pat down. During this time, the culture was such that knives were frequently carried, so that in itself it was not out of the ordinary. Approximately a minute after the car was stopped, Providence HQ dispatched cars for a multiple stabbing that had taken place at a nearby bar. Shortly after the officers arrived on the scene, they put out a description of the suspects involved, who were, in fact, the individuals we had stopped. We handcuffed the suspects and, upon closer examination of the knives, saw that there was blood on them. Unfortunately, one of the victims ended up dying from his wounds, but because of good, proactive patrol work by the Providence police officers, the murder suspects were captured, and the murder weapons recovered. This is also a good time to address the people who frequently make snide comments when more than one patrol car is present at a car stop. In this case, nobody will know, but had we not had an overwhelming presence of officers there and there was only one officer, what might the three occupants have done to escape?

Before, citizens make comments such as "Three cop cars had one car stopped. What a waste of time. They should be out catching criminals."

They should consider what the job involves. When you go in for surgery, I don't think you complain about too many doctors and other staff being present, do you?

In the same vein, there is another famous line heard from the uninformed: "It took three of them to handcuff the guy."

I would challenge anyone to handcuff an actively resistive subject by themselves, without causing extensive injury to the suspect and yourself. It often takes multiple officers to handcuff a resistive suspect. This not only minimizes injury to the officers but also minimizes injury to the suspect as well. Lt. Dan Evans responded to a similar comment one time with a great line: "When they pay me what professional fighters get to go one-on-one with a suspect, then I will too. Until then, I'm going home at night."

As I will mention further in another chapter, traffic control and traffic stops are a means of preventing motor-vehicle crashes, thus preserving life and property. They are also a means of identifying criminal activity that may be going on in your community. If officers are issuing a high number of traffic violations yet their arrest rate is low, it may be time for some intervention. It could be a coincidence, but maybe the officer is not making arrests to avoid the paperwork involved. Depending on the mind-set of the administration, this officer might think they are doing the right thing by keeping the crime rate low while building the city's coffers.

The duties of a patrol officer will constantly be changing. The only way to deal with these changes is to be patrolling out on the streets. There are some studies that state that the presence of or lack thereof of police officers on the street have no bearing on the crime rate. I don't believe these studies one bit. I have always heard from citizens in general: "You never see a cop drive by" or, the opposite, "Whenever you go through (your city) there is a cop on every corner."

I believe wholeheartedly that the law-abiding citizens of your community want to see police presence in their neighborhood. I also believe the criminal element does not want to see this presence and will come up with a variety of complaints to discourage it. Knowing what your job as a patrol officer is, what do you think? As a citizen, what are your feelings on this?

CHAPTER

10

# PATROL OPERATIONS

# CREATIVE PROBLEM-SOLVING

As I stated previously in this book, there is such a wide variety of situations you will encounter while on patrol that there is no way you can have a guideline, policy, or procedure to deal with them all, nor should your department attempt to be that micromanaged. As patrol officers, Captain Broadmeadow and I were assigned one midnight to locate a polar bear that had just escaped from a local zoo. No policy, no training—just improvise. Thankfully, we were not the ones who found it. If we did, I am not sure what we would have done. I don't think our .38 caliber pistols or even our shotguns with buck shot would have been much help. The point is you are not going to have a standard operating procedure (SOP) for every situation you are going to encounter. You need to be doing "problem-solving policing." This is what all police officers should be doing all the time. I don't think we need some new policy or theory to shape and mold it. Another term that might better be used is *common sense*. If I could ever bottle and patent this, I would be a gazillionaire. The fact is that most people have common sense, but unfortunately, there is a good portion of those that don't. This is one thing departments should be looking at during the entry-level screening, not sex, race, size, glasses, sexual orientation, etc., but how much common sense does the candidate have.

Think outside of the box. Think outside of the box. Think outside of the box. You don't need to go to a seminar to think outside of the box. Just think outside of the box. I could write volumes on situations I and others have handled that were not spelled out in our department's policies and procedures. I will try and relay some of the more humorous and practical ones throughout this book as examples, but remember, your mission is the good of the public.

In patrol operations, patrol officers and their supervisors should be allowed and encouraged to engage in unorthodox techniques. During my career, patrol officers were frequently assigned to be in plain clothes, use unmarked vehicles, bicycles, etc. With twelve miles of coastline, we never had a boat, yet when one was needed, it didn't take long to get one. It was not always the fire department boat either; many of our local boat owners were more than willing to take us out in their boat when we needed their assistance. Don't be afraid to ask the citizens to assist you with your task. They often have equipment that could help you in dealing with unique situations. Construction companies have some great equipment that we used from time to time. Cpl. Fred George and I once sought the assistance of an engineer to take us on a freight train to a remote industrial area to check on something. Okay, maybe we were being lazy and thought it would be cool to drive in the locomotive, but the point was he was more than willing to assist us and take us to that remote area. As well as saving us a long walk in the heat, we built another positive relationship with someone in our community. We now had a new set of eyes who, through his job, was frequently in one of the more remote areas of our city.

If you want to get a true feeling of what is going on in an area, assign two officers in plain clothes on bicycles (not marked "POLICE") to patrol that area. I had the pleasure of doing this several times with my partner at the time, Capt. Walter Barlow, while assigned to the fluid patrol unit. This was a real eye opener for both of us, especially during the early morning hours. You were able to patrol with such stealth. It is amazing what you will see and hear. This was a great way of interdicting street-level drug sales and use. It also served as a great tool in targeted crime areas.

One such case of targeted crime involved the apprehension of a burglar who had plagued an area for two years, breaking into homes while the occupants slept. Because of this, we were assigned to this area on bicycles from eight in the evening to four in the morning. Around three in the morning, a call for a house break came in. As soon as the call came in, we went to the area that we assumed he was using for an escape route. Moments after arriving there, we heard him lumber over a wooden bridge within a golf course. Seconds after this, we spotted him slinking along a fence, and the foot chase was on. Had the officers working at that time been the only ones trying to locate him, we may never have done so.

Fortunately, the officer in charge was Capt. David Allsworth, a lieutenant at the time. Within minutes, not hours, not waiting for approval from the chief, he began a massive callback of off-duty officers to saturate the area. Within an hour, we had over half the police department staking out this area. His focus was not on how much overtime it would cost but on capturing a dangerous criminal who was definitely having a negative impact on the quality of life for many residents in the north end of our city. As a result of his decisive actions and the tenacity of all the officers involved, approximately four hours later, he was apprehended. It happened when less than a block from where the suspect was originally spotted, Cpl. Robert Rock heard some unusual breathing near a brook. Upon closer inspection, he found the suspect lying submerged in the brook, using a reed as a snorkel. Corporal Rock and others quickly arrested the subject and, as a result, solved multiple felonies.

The first Thanksgiving on the job, I was scheduled to work the four-to-twelve shift, so I had a nice large meal and planned on being a reactive patrol officer all night, parked in one place, digesting. The only problems with my plans, however, were the plans of the officer working the next post that night. Lt. John Lynch did not plan on having a reactive evening. He taught me the value of parking a car and walking through a busy parking lot of a local club. We made three separate drug busts that evening. I learned the full advantage of getting out of the car, walking in stealth, and being observant. I am sure every jurisdiction has a similar location that can result in similar results. Yes, the crime rate went up, but in the long run, this soon became NOT the place to do your dope in the car. This is yet another example of problem-solving policing at its best.

One night when I was working as the midnight-shift lieutenant, Sgt. John Burney who had recently transferred from detectives to patrol told me that one of his informants had just called him with information about someone trying to sell some stolen goods from a local company. At two in the morning, we needed to act quickly as there were no detectives working. With very little time and only nine officers working, we were able to get Sgt. Mike Rose to go undercover, dress up as a wise guy, and make contact with the suspect. After the transaction, the suspect was arrested, and as a result of this, our department recovered thousands of dollars' worth of stolen goods and helped identify the source of what had been an ongoing loss for this company.

In all these cases, we could have easily said that it was not our job at the time and forward it to the appropriate division for follow-up. The fact is the sooner you act upon a criminal activity, the more likely you will be successful in stopping it and apprehending the people responsible. It is much easier to catch and convict someone caught in the act than through follow-up investigation, regardless of how talented your investigators are. In the case above, it was much easier for detectives to do a thorough investigation of all the thefts, having a suspect in custody, along with a large amount of seized stolen property.

Another tactic we employed often when staffing allowed was to take two patrol officers and put them in plain clothes in an unmarked car (the "Shapiro van" for those who remember, a throwaway vehicle from the *Vice Squad*). Sometimes they were sent to areas of target crimes, and other times they were encouraged to just patrol. In the hundreds of times we did this, I could count on one hand the number of shifts they did not make an arrest. This assignment served multiple purposes. It allowed us to place officers in target crime areas undercover, increasing the likelihood of an arrest. It provided officers with a little variation from their routine schedule. Officers who were assigned to a regular post could now focus on some of the problem areas from a plain-clothes perspective and solve some of the problems they could not while in a marked cruiser. The most important benefit was that word got around on the street of what we were doing. Criminals talk to one another, and it allowed for a deserved feeling of paranoia among our street criminals knowing we were likely patrolling the area in an unmarked car.

Another very creative plan we employed was done by Capt. Bill Sloyer and Maj. Wayne Gallagher, sergeants at the time, along with the shift commander Capt. Dennis McCarthy. During this era, milk-store robberies were becoming a problem in our city. Under their direction, unoccupied cruisers were parked adjacent to some milk stores, while other milk stores had two officers assigned to sit in the back cooler to observe the store. After many weeks, eventually, an arrest was made. Word got out on the street of our tactics, and milk-store robberies ceased. I know many of you young people are saying, "Why not put in a video camera?" The point is this: we did we not have video cameras readily available to us, but what we had were creative supervisors who were able to quickly develop a tactic, deviating from the norm and implementing it. It did not require committees, think tanks, lengthy meetings, or overall department approval. It was a creative plan supported department-wide that worked.

Do you think you might need help with your creativity? If so and even if you don't think so, I encourage you to stop taking selfies and playing mindless games on your cell phone and browse through your state and local laws. You will be amazed at what you find and then realize that you can apply these laws to your probable cause. We had a group of skinheads (neo-Nazis) move into one of our neighborhoods one time, and obviously, it created a stir with the local residents. As offensive as I find their ideology, it is not against the law for a group such as this to have a "headquarters" in a neighborhood until they take some type of overt action. Now while the local politicians were holding meeting after meeting, promising to pass new laws (which I'm sure would have been unconstitutional), the police took action. Remember the nuisance issue in the previous chapter? We applied those principles. While the officers assigned to patrol regularly monitored this location, my fellow detectives and I got together and came up with another plan. We realized that many members of this group were now sporting new tattoos proclaiming their ideology. Tattoos are not illegal, but it was a crime at the time to tattoo a person under the age of eighteen, which many of these members were. With the help of a confidential informant, we learned that certain members of this group were the ones actually tattooing these minors inside of their headquarters. Based on this information, we got a search warrant, with the scope to find evidence relating to tattooing of minors. When we executed the search warrant, we found the evidence of tattooing minors, along with weapons, Molotov cocktails, and detailed written plans on how to conduct criminal assaults on certain ethnic groups of people.

It was also a crime in the state of Rhode Island to disturb and destroy natural flora. This one came in quite handy when we found a low-level wise guy digging a grave in a very remote location of our city, damaging the natural flora in the process. This flower crime gave us probable cause to arrest him, tow the car, and do an inventory search of the trunk. A subsequent warrant allowed us to check for residue blood. No body nor blood was found, but an obscure law, along with some creative problem-solving, allowed us to intervene. Hopefully, we prevented a murder. Regardless, the criminal element knew they were on our radar, and I'm sure some higher ups in the organization were not happy with their underling.

Creativity should follow you up the ladder. While working as patrol sergeant one midnight shift, we had a snowstorm quickly turn into a major blizzard. We only had one four-wheel-drive police vehicle available for eight officers. Obviously, this was going to be a problem for us responding to calls and patrolling. Prior to roll call, I noticed that many of the officers were all arriving at work, driving in with their personal four-wheel-drive vehicles. After a quick conversation with Lieutenant Trail, we offered these officers an option. They could use their own four-wheel-drive vehicles, get a full tank of gas at the beginning and at the end of the shift. It was totally voluntary, yet all agreed. The shift went well; everyone went home safe, and they were still able to provide services to the community. Our focus was on officer safety and public service. Our focus was not on the cost of fuel or a liability analysis of officers using personal vehicles. As always, the next day, when the administration came in, the idea was supported. You need to be able to quickly solve problems, but your administration needs to foster that type of thinking.

I could tell hundreds of these bizarre stories that most people would not believe, other than the police officers who have encountered them. I want to conclude by saying that whenever officers operated outside of the box at my department, for the most part, they were supported all the way up the chain of command. Creative problem-solving was a culture that was nurtured at the East Providence Police Department, and it resulted in a great clearance rate and true crime deterrence. This is one of those community-policing concepts that works when applied department-wide. It does not require the decision-making be hierarchal but gives officers the responsibility and authority to act upon situations quickly when a problem presents itself and then the support of administrators to encourage these types of actions. If your department does not foster such an environment, then I encourage you to do so.

CHAPTER

**11**

# PATROL OPERATIONS

# BASIC INVESTIGATIONS IN PATROL

## A. THE INVESTIGATION OF PROPERTY CRIMES

I don't want to get into too many details of investigating specific crimes in this book, but most departments are likely to have to deal with a high volume of theft reports. I include this under patrol operations because I believe how a department handles theft reports has a great impact on the quality of policing, the crime rate, and the overall community perception of the police department. Let us look at the following example.

Sally Smith comes home from work; it is already dark. When she opens her front door, she realizes that someone has broken into her house. She then calls 911. The dispatcher asks if the intruder is there now. When Sally says no, the dispatcher transfers her to a records clerk who then proceeds to take the breaking and entering report over the telephone. Or, Sally is directed to a website where she can directly report the crime online. If Sally asks to speak with a police officer she is told that the department's policy allows for people to conveniently report burglaries over the phone, or online. Sally is then directed to some form of artificial intelligence (AI) that generates a case number and then asks her a series of predetermined questions about the burglary. Sally then proceeds to answer these questions. Upon completing this process, the AI informs Sally of her case number and then automatically enters the data into the department's system where it can be accessed for future reference.

Do you think this is a good way to serve a member of the public who has been a victim of a crime? If you said no, you are correct. If you agree with this, let me tell you that this is wrong in so many ways. Can you guess why based on what you have read so far? This type of policy with varying criteria has been implemented in police departments throughout the country for years. The underlying philosophy is this will free up officers to be on the street. Again, I don't know for sure, but my guess is this started with some criminal justice expert with a large degree and no street time in patrol.

Let us examine this scenario from a police officer's perspective. Sally has no idea if the criminal is still in the house. The dispatcher should have advised her to leave the house immediately until an officer arrived who would check the house to make sure the criminal or criminals had, in fact, left. Ideally, two officers are dispatched to the house to check it. They should check every nook and cranny of her home where a criminal could be hiding. Once they determine the house is clear of intruders, an officer needs to start the investigation. What evidence does the officer see to start documenting the investigation? The officer needs to establish a rapport with Sally and start asking questions related to this specific incident, not from a computer-generated list of boilerplate questions, some of which may have no relevance to this particular crime. While the officer is there, Sally will now have a period of some security as her adrenaline levels start to lower. She may relax enough to remember some recent event that may help the police in developing a suspect. The officer can relay to her the need of preserving the crime scene until such time as the crime scene investigators arrive. In the end, the officers have been good ambassadors for the department while working to solve a criminal act. Hopefully, the officer's actions have provided Sally with a positive image of her local police agency.

And to respond to that eggheaded idea that "call in reporting" keeps officers on the streets, let me say this: What are they on the street for? I am sure even in the deluded world of criminal-justice academia, the answer is to suppress crime. Well, let me state the obvious: *crime* is caused by criminals. The officer responding to that call is on the *street*, more specifically, right on a specific street at an exact location where a criminal was not that long ago or, if you are lucky, may still be. So what better place to begin your search for criminals than where they were recently. Who knows, you might immediately find some evidence of who the criminal was so you can focus your search rather than drive around aimlessly. If you sense a tone of frustration on my part, you are correct. Officers all over the world are forced to compromise their profession while some idiotic social experiment that endangers the public is played out.

The long-term effect of a policy such as this is devastating. People are placed in unnecessary danger. Sally may have interrupted the criminal, so he hid in a closet. Once cornered, the intruder will become more likely to commit violence in order to escape and avoid detection. By not having an officer present, her level of security will likely be impacted, and she will be less likely to look at her police agency as a means of protection. Her overall view of the police department and the profession in general is likely to deteriorate.

From an officer's viewpoint, if they are not required to go to a crime scene in person, they will not be honing their tactical, investigative, and interpersonal skills. They will not be getting to know the people who live on their beat and not learn to become the department's ambassadors. They may, in fact, become lazy, and when something serious confronts them in the future, they may fail because of the lack of good policies and actual experience.

It also does not take long for the criminal element to realize such a policy exists. Knowing that officers are not going to respond to a crime scene means that no evidence will be secured (unless Sally brings the piece of broken glass dripping with blood to the police station). So even though they might not have a degree in criminal justice, they are able to deduce that no evidence equates to the unlikelihood of identification and apprehension. I think it is a reasonable assumption that crime is going to increase when a policy such as this exists.

If you are an administrator who implemented or would implement such a policy, shame on you! Find a new profession. It is obvious that you are a numbers person and are not interested in providing a safe community the best trained officers you can have. Yes, you will certainly be able to justify a cut in officers assigned to patrol and probably a cut in staff overall, but what about the public good? If this scenario happened at the mayor's or your parents' or your children's house, would you tell them to just call it in? I doubt it. I can see you personally getting off your butt, responding to the scene and overseeing all the officers conducting the investigation at Mayor Smith's house. If, in fact, you really think this is a good idea, you really need to quit. You are a disgrace to the millions of men and women who have worn their shields with pride.

Another common incidence of theft you will encounter is when a child's bicycle or skateboard is stolen. I agree this is not the crime of the century and is truly not something you look forward to investigating, but think of it from a child's perspective. This is one of their prized possessions that allow them a sense of freedom. You are the department's ambassador, and this is a key moment in building that relationship. Recovering a stolen item for a child goes a long way into building that positive relationship, maybe for a lifetime, not only with the child but also with their family and friends as well. This goes beyond recovering bicycles. I, along with all the officers I worked with, recovered stolen articles all the time and were able to eventually return them to the owner. I never once had a victim tell me they did not care about the fact we recovered the item. On the contrary, most were quite ecstatic and very thankful for our efforts.

On the flip side, this is an ideal time to identify your future criminals. Is it merely a childhood prank, or is this a young upcoming criminal honing his skills? Does it involve threats and intimidation? Is the young criminal starting a little criminal enterprise, a chop shop for bikes for resale? Hopefully, you can encourage the young thief to walk a different path in life, but at least you can get the young criminal's data into the system, including fingerprints where allowed, to help solve future crimes and identify those who will be committing them.

Crimes against property are certainly not as serious as crimes against a person. Police officers know this, and once they realize no one is dead or injured, they tend to move this toward the back of their priority list. The fact remains that most citizens will have their first contact with the police department as a result of a property crime. Seize on the moment to be the department's ambassador, hone your investigative skills, and solve the crime.

## B. MISSING PERSONS

Missing-person reports are another area that patrol officers are going to encounter on a frequent basis. In this day and age, please don't have that lazy line: "Yeah, we got to wait twenty-four hours before taking a missing person's report."

I am not sure where this idea came from—from an urban myth, the television, a poor administrative policy, or some lazy cop who didn't feel like taking a report. Regardless, this "wait twenty-four hours" is the perception that a lot of people still have in relation to whether they should file a missing-person report. As a police officer, when someone reports a missing person to you, this is not the time to figure out how you can get out of a report and pass the buck on for another twenty-four hours. This is the time to use your common sense and your investigative skills. If, in fact, foul play is involved, a lot can happen in twenty-four hours. Do you want to take the responsibility for no action taking place for twenty-four hours? Now is the time for you to ask who, what, when, where, WHY, and how. After you get the basics, the big question should by why. Is it a custodial case? Is the missing person someone whom kidnappers might want to hold for hostage because of the financial ability to pay ransom of someone close to them? Is the missing person a witness in an upcoming criminal case? Is it totally out of character for this person to be missing at a point in time when someone contacts the police? As a rule, people just don't randomly call the police because Eddy is not home from work at the usual time. Usually, circumstances and timing make the reporting party feel that something is wrong. Just as you rely on your sixth sense, don't ignore others when they feel something is wrong.

Even after presuming foul play is not the reason someone is missing, officers need to consider, without waiting twenty-four hours, what the missing person's mental state is. Do they have a new romantic partner whom they are off with? Is it a child in fear of punishment for something they did? Are they suffering from Alzheimer's or dementia? Are they on a new medication that will affect their ability to reason or cause them to get confused? The questions are endless.

If it is a child or young adult still living at home, check the house, even if the reporting party tells you they already checked it. Ptl. John Cialella instilled this procedure into me, and so often the missing child was, in fact, hiding somewhere in the house. If the reporting party is reluctant to have you check the house, again your sixth sense should be alerted. Use some common sense at this point and explain to the reporting party that you are not concerned about the bag of dope that may be sitting on the table, but your primary concern is the well-being of the missing person. Give them the option to go "check the house again" before you come in. (The well-being of an endangered child outweighs a narcotics arrest.) If after this option is given and there is still reluctance on the part of the reporting party to let you search the building for the missing person, you need to start focusing on how to get into that house legally. Let's be realistic. Most homicides are committed by someone connected to the victim, including parents and children. Your obligation is to that missing person, and you need to act in a manner that puts their well-being as a priority. I say do it legally because if you just force your way in and find evidence of a murder, you are going to have a tough time introducing it as evidence. Know the laws in your community, and be aware of what actions you can and can't do legally.

Once the basic information about the missing person is secured, disseminate it as soon as possible. Continue your investigation at the scene while other officers can start the search. Once the reports are finalized, your department should have a method in place that disseminates this information beyond your department. Social media and AMBER alerts are two of the most efficient ways. In days past, we had flyers of missing persons that would come in from a multitude of agencies with no central database to reach out to. Yes, the FBI had a central database, but it was not user-friendly, nor did it contain pertinent data that could be disseminated easily to the public.

Missing-person reports are going to be a part of your daily routine. Learn to properly handle these investigations early in your career. Although the vast majority of these cases will end up being a young child running away from home to go down the street to their friend's house because they got a D on their report card, don't automatically assume that is the case when you are taking the initial report. A successful closure of these cases in a timely manner can save lives.

# CHAPTER 12

# PATROL OPERATIONS

# CULTURAL AWARENESS

The United States of America is probably one of the most diverse countries in the world. If you are in doubt, take a look at the ethnic makeup of our Olympic teams compared with those of other countries. As a law enforcement officer, you need to be aware of what cultures are living in your community and how you can best serve them as a representative of your department. Your community will be enhanced by these cultures and their various gifts and talents, but don't be blinded by political correctness. In addition to the enhancements, certain cultures are going to bring certain problems to your community. Be aware of the problems that these groups can bring to your community. As my father-in-law, at the time an immigrant from Portugal, once said, "You are not always getting the successful members of a particular culture moving into your community." A perfect example would be when Cuba's Fidel Castro emptied his prisons and mental hospitals and complied with President Carter's request to allow Cubans the freedom to go to the United States of America. Castro gave them a one-way pass to the USA, and my guess would be with a big smile on his face. This certainly required us to learn about their culture, particularly what their prison tattoos stood for. By the way, most of the tattoos were not for public drunkenness.

The fact is this is the United States of America, and we should welcome other cultures with open arms. This country was built on a great mix of peoples and continues to do so. Both of my grandmothers were illegal aliens, yet they were very proud of this country and verbally expressed it frequently. All their sons joined the United States military. The problem arises when new cultural traditions conflict with our laws. You should at all times be culturally sensitive, but don't become politically correct, ignorant, or naive. Remember, the criminal element will often prey on their own community first, so it is imperative that you have established a good rapport with each unique community in your municipality to prevent the organized criminals within a group from gaining hold. You also need to be aware of how the police are perceived in the country from where they come from. Sadly, some foreign police departments are viewed in a negative light by their citizens, often for good reason. They are viewed as being (or maybe they are) an extension of the military often run by a dictator. These people are not fleeing their countries because they are living the dream there and just want to change it up. A lot of them are terrified. And then there are some of them who are looking to establish or expand their criminal empire by finding a fresh batch of victims, starting with the weakest in their own community. You need to show these groups through actions that the police department is not their enemy and that they can call upon the police when victimized. The way you are going to demonstrate this is to be out on the street. Patronize their stores, restaurants, etc., and get to know the community and let them get to know you. Don't depend on the fabricated meet and greets to establish these relationships because often they are political ploys to keep the politicians who want nothing more than a photo op happy. Take advantage of these meet and greets and use your investigative skills to see who keeps organizing these meetings. If they are not involved in criminal activity themselves, they are more than likely to know who makes up the criminal element within their community. If they are not relaying this information to law enforcement, then what is their motive for not doing so? Do they just want to look good to the members of their community, or is their motive more nefarious? Are they encouraging the administration to "back off" a little so their criminal enterprise can flourish while gathering intelligence on law enforcement operations?

Cultural sensitivity does not mean ignoring the enforcement of the laws you have been sworn to uphold. I was in attendance at a cultural-sensitivity training seminar when I was told that a certain Asian culture treats ill children by cutting the child's face, and this should be expected. We had a rather long discussion about cultural traditions versus child abuse. Unfortunately, for all in attendance, most of the session remained on this topic, but I felt it was important to not back down and stand for principles. It is not okay for people to scar their children's faces to heal them in the United States of America. Period. We are a nation of laws, and just as those laws protect all, all are expected to live by them. When in Rome, do as the Romans. When in the United State of America, do as Americans do. This is a point to focus on. If you believe in something, stand for that principle. Don't compromise. This is that portion of policing where it may not always be comfortable, easy, or timely to stand for what is right, but it is the right thing to do.

My younger brother has the honor of serving with the United States Army and, at one point, was assigned to a special unit in Iraq. The unit was purposely made up of a minority of Americans and included equal numbers of Shiite, Sunni, and Kurdish Iraqi soldiers. Based on my conversations with him, this was cultural integration at its best. The bottom line, he would tell me, is they all are regular people trying to make ends meet to support their families.

Did they all like one another? No! Did they all respect one other and work toward a common goal? Yes!

This demonstrates the fact that a group of people with a history of intolerance toward one another can coexist. How much more should different cultures in our society coexist? And you as a law enforcement officer need to facilitate this. This is done by treating all people equally. Amendment XIV of the United States Constitution includes within it the following line: "Nor to deny to any person within its jurisdiction the EQUAL protection of the law."

*Equal* means that all should receive the same treatment. If you question where some resentment toward the police comes from within certain communities, look at the way the law is enforced. Sadly, some people with money and political clout get a pass on criminal behavior. And I'm not just talking about speeding tickets but some very serious crimes. I'm sure you all are familiar with some famous public figure who flagrantly violated the law and got away with it. Economic status, race, creed, religion, sexual orientation, gender should never be a consideration when enforcing the law. If you are going to give the rich white guy a break for a certain crime, then you need to do the same for the poor black guy. On the other hand, criminal activity should not be ignored based on these factors either. Nothing turns sentiment against law enforcement more than when a certain group gets preferential treatment. You may get a lot of public attention for arresting politically connected Richie Rich, but if you don't arrest him, you are going to get a lot more behind-the-scenes attention from the community as a whole. The community that you have worked to gain their trust and expect them to assist you in your mission needs to see you are a person they can, in fact, trust. Politics has no business interfering with the day-to-day operation of a police department. Elected officials need to provide oversight about the overall operation of the department, and that's where it needs to end.

If you treat people differently based on their race, socioeconomic status, etc., you are not going to earn their respect. Simple. On the flip side, if you are going to give a break to someone, think about the citizens who are just about making it in life. John Smith needs his car to get to his two jobs that he works at every day. He forgot to register the car because of his schedule. When you stop John and find out this information, what are your choices? By law, you can issue him a violation and have his car towed. If you do this, realize how this is going to affect his life. His financial burden just increased. The other option, maybe not authorized in your department, is to use some discretion. Verbally tell John Smith he has so many days to register the car and correct the problem, or else . . . If you decide to do this, check on John Smith in the time frame you gave him to make sure he has handled the problem. If he has not, "or else." The fact is John Smith is more than likely to correct the problems based on your request. This is one of those moments where you are using common sense and are being a good ambassador. I am sure that if it did not reach the "or else" level, John Smith will be more than willing to become a lifelong advocate for the mission of your department.

I hope your department is one that allows all its citizens to flourish and encourages equal enforcement of the laws. If not, it is up to you to follow that principle and set an example.

CHAPTER

13

# INVESTIGATIVE SERVICES

A s I mentioned before, all police officers should be investigators; however, when you get assigned to a specialized investigative unit, your focus will change. Detectives and vice, traffic, and crime scene specialists are just some of the specialized units that exist within police departments. Some of the larger departments will break these areas down further and have additional units such as cybercrime units, gang units, antiterrorist units. I encourage administrators and investigators not to get too specialized. Administrators should ask themselves this question: Is the need for this specialized unit a reflection of the overall breakdown of basic policing within your department? Remember your basic duty—to preserve life and property. You want to have enough officers available to investigate the daily workload of crime. Don't have too many officers focusing on a particular crime while the other officers are overwhelmed in their workload. And if you are in one of these specialized units, maybe with not a lot to do and are being a "house mouse," don't spend your time Monday morning quarterbacking those officers who are overwhelmed with the other investigations.

When you are assigned to an investigative unit, you get to apply all that investigating experience you gained as a patrol officer in a specialized field. Again, there are hundreds of books that deal with various investigative techniques. Depending upon the focus of your unit, you should seek out this information and increase your knowledge in that field of expertise. Another way to expand your knowledge base is to work with experienced investigators in your field. Nothing will give you the experience as much as working on a case with a more experienced investigator. If you have a case that you need help with, swallow your pride and reach out to them. I have found that most trained investigators are more than willing to share their expertise. It boosts their esteem—a good thing—and you will likely gain new knowledge in your field. More than likely, you will also be able to teach them something new. Just don't hold your breath, waiting for them to tell you that you did.

As an investigator, I encourage you to reach out to officers conducting similar investigations in outside agencies when conducting your investigations. Again you will be sharing information and skills, and in the end, you are more likely to solve the crime while becoming a better investigator. I encourage you to participate in associations that promote interagency relationships. Don't ever be so narrow-minded to think problems in neighboring communities don't impact your community. Criminals certainly don't pay attention to municipal boundaries, that is, unless your department has a reputation in the criminal community that encourages them NOT to commit crimes in your jurisdiction. That is a nice compliment, and it is demonstrative that your agency is doing things right, but you are still going to have interjurisdictional crime.

How specialized your investigative units will depend upon the size of your department, demographics, and specific needs. However, remember that one type of crime is not exclusive of the others, especially in this day and age. My guess would be drug and alcohol misuse and addiction would account for about 90 percent of the crime we suffer in America. As an investigator, you need to have a general knowledge of the current trends that impact criminal activity. What is the latest drug of choice? What is the latest scam? What groups are active in your community? The fact that you are in a specialized unit does not mean you should forget the basics. All soldiers are not assigned to the infantry, but all soldiers know how to handle and fire a rifle.

Regardless of the size of your department, your department needs the ability to have officers trained and become specialists in specific areas, even if the bulk of their time will be on the street in patrol. These need to be officers who once trained in an area of expertise and who can then focus on a specific investigation for a specific time, that is, they can work exclusively on an investigation without having to handle calls for service in the meantime.

I will stick in the overtime factor here. When a serious crime occurs, this is not the time to balance the budget. If you really need to, there is plenty of fluff to trim within your department, but don't impede investigations that will allow people to remain in peril for longer periods because your overtime budget is exhausted.

If you reported your child missing to the police and when you called for an update, you were told all the officers with knowledge of the case went home because the department was cutting back on the budget, how would you feel? The critics will say I am personalizing this. Well, yes, I am making it personal because that is exactly what it is to that family—very personal. Just like any other crime, it is personal to the victims. To the pinheaded folks in academia who look at nothing but numbers, this could pose a problem to your formula. For the people who are experiencing this, it is a crisis, and they rightly want their police department to act quickly. Whenever a life is in danger, your department needs to be able to drop the mundane and focus its resources to preserve life. Information needs to be passed on to other officers—at least it should be. This is imperative. The officers working the case are the ones who have firsthand knowledge and can properly coordinate the efforts with the rest of the department. This includes passing on pertinent information so that a victim never receives an answer such as "I don't know. Call back tomorrow."

For supervisors and administrators, there needs to be ONE officer assigned to the case. You obviously are going to have other officers assisting, maybe the entire department, but ONE officer needs to be assigned to the case. This is basic incident command, authority, and responsibility. If the officer is not properly handling the case, then assign it to another officer and make the change clear to all involved. It can be done very diplomatically, but do it. Don't let an officer handle a case who is unable to do so, while others do the work. It is not fair to all involved, especially the victim and the officers doing all the work.

Charles E. O'Hara's book *Fundamentals of Criminal Investigation* describes the basic tools of an investigation as being "the three *Is*"— information, interrogation, and instrumentation. The book is extremely dated and briefly covers some investigations that are inappropriate and archaic in this day and age, but the basics of investigations remain the same. Should you decide to read it, use your creativity and problem-solving skills to apply the modern science and technology we have today to enhance the investigative techniques he describes in his book.

I will further cover some of the specific investigative units in other chapters, but regardless of what investigative unit you are assigned, remember the basics of policing. You are working for the public good, and your mission is to provide for the good of the public by solving and preventing crime.

# TRAFFIC SERVICES

Traffic service is an integral part of any police department, and it is going to have a strong investigative component. It is not simply handing out speeding tickets and parking tickets and writing up accident reports. Regardless of the size of your municipality, your police department needs to be monitoring the traffic that occurs within it. Traffic services encompass the flow and control of traffic, enforcement of violations of the established traffic controls, and investigations related to traffic accidents. Traffic law enforcement and investigations should be the responsibility of all uniformed police officers, even if a specialized unit exists.

Lt. Robert McKenna did an excellent job creating our department's general orders. Some of the orders relating to traffic were as follows:

> *Traffic enforcement.* The purpose of this policy is to establish procedures for traffic law enforcement activities, including general and specialized enforcement, traffic stops, physical arrests, summons, and procedures. It is the policy to protect lives and property of people using the highways, through professional and impartial traffic enforcement. Furthermore, it is the policy to promote safe and expeditious flow of vehicular and pedestrian traffic through effective and efficient traffic-related services and enforcement designed to reduce collisions and their resultant fatalities and injuries.

If your department is large enough, you should have a separate unit focusing on traffic. If not, you should have officers who are delegated the responsibility of monitoring traffic issues within your municipality. This monitoring needs to include the review of all traffic accidents; identifying where, when, dates, days, times, weather, etc.; and, hopefully, determining why. It should also review all traffic violations issued, or the lack thereof, asking the same set of questions. There also needs to be a means of reviewing and analyzing civilian complaints that relate to traffic.

I have mentioned a uniformed appearance enough, so I think you get the idea that like all uniformed officers, traffic officers should look sharp. Most officers assigned to a traffic unit have some form of identification on their uniforms, indicating their specialty.

As mentioned above, the goal of traffic enforcement is "to promote the safe and expeditious flow of vehicular and pedestrian traffic through effective and efficient traffic-related services and enforcement designed to reduce collisions and their resultant fatalities and injuries."

It does not state "to supplement the municipalities budget by generating new funds through aggressive traffic enforcement because we, the elected officials, have poorly planned the budgetary needs of this municipality."

One of the problems with traffic enforcement is how it is viewed by administrators and elected officials. If they view it as a cash cow, then your police department is not serving the public good. I, unfortunately, have seen this time after time. I am a strong advocate for aggressive traffic enforcement. I believe a long-term, aggressive approach to traffic enforcement program reduces the number of accidents and injuries. Your department should be known for its traffic enforcement. A neighboring community to ours had one of the most aggressive traffic programs in the state. It had a reputation for being tough on violations, and it had a drastically low number of fatal accidents. That should be the goal of targeted traffic enforcement. It should not be the goal to set up a radar trap in the area where the speed limit drops quickly from forty miles per hour to twenty-five miles per hour in a short period to increase the number of violations issued. This is an area where common sense needs to be applied by police officers. A verbal warning can often be much more effective than a written violation in obtaining your goal. Written warnings are an even more effective tool that allows officers to use some discretion yet still tracks data. If the same violator has received numerous written warnings, then violations can be issued.

Another area of concern relating to traffic and the promotion of the cash cow is the municipalities that hire outside agencies or civilians to enforce traffic laws—most notably, parking violations. Again, another moneymaker for the municipality. Traffic enforcement, including parking violations, should be done by police officers, and all uniformed police officers should be responsible for what happens on their beat. If your municipality has been so poorly planned to not have sufficient parking available for the people going into your community, then assign police officers the task of parking violations. As mentioned, police officers can apply common sense to a situation and not ticket everybody. While they are out enforcing parking laws, they can be a part of the community and learn about all the "quality of life" issues the people in the neighborhood are dealing with. Officers can also use their investigative skills for each car they approach. Does the car have a damage? Is it reported stolen? Is their contraband within? Is there blood around the trunk? These questions may seem stupid, but is a civilian meter enforcement employee going to notice things like this, or are they simply concerned about getting their quota of tickets in order to keep their job? These questions are second nature to patrol officers. I realize patrol officers are not wild about enforcing parking violations, but it is part of their job. If you have a major problem in your municipality with parking problems, put more police officers on the streets; don't send out a group of civilians at minimum wage. There have even been cases of volunteer traffic enforcement officers handing out parking tickets. I remember a group of them approaching Chief Winquist one time about instituting this program in our city to enforce handicap plate violations. Of course, his answer was no as this was a disaster waiting to happen.

For all the non–law enforcement people still reading, I will tell you what parking violations are going to get a beat officer's attention: parking in a handicap spot without a valid sticker (or if you have a sticker and sprint into the store), parking in a crosswalk, parking in front of a fire hydrant (aside from the ticket, this is a great way to have your windows smashed out and a leaking hose draped across your interior of your car for hours), and obstructing an intersection. You can gamble with the others, but these fall under that category of protecting life and property, and you are very likely to get ticketed.

Traffic services will have officers trained in a variety of specialties, most notably accident reconstruction and commercial vehicle enforcement. Each of these requires additional training and equipment. Officers assigned to traffic should be able to work closely with your municipality's public works and planning departments as a means of gathering information and providing suggestions. They should also have contacts with the state agencies that provide oversight of traffic related matters. If you establish these relationships, you are going to have not only great insight but also great input into the overall operation of traffic control and planning. Many times, traffic officers attended meetings at the state department of transportation and, based on their input, were able to have installed, modified, or removed permanent traffic control devices. Often the people involved in these agencies do not have the same experience that a police officer will have on what happens daily at a specific intersection, section of roadway, etc. If your traffic officers present their concerns in a professional manner, supported by well-written police reports, their input will be appreciated and considered.

As a citizen, you can easily identify the people who are responsible for speeding up and down your street. Look in the mirror. How do you drive in your neighborhood? If you drive with care, do you take that same attitude to the other neighborhoods you drive through? It was almost inevitable that the ones complaining the most about speeding vehicles were the same ones speeding in their own neighborhood. One such case was when Corporal DeAquair and I were directed by the chief to monitor speeding on Turner Avenue from four to five thirty in the afternoon every day. We were not wild about the daily assignment, but we did it. One day, one of the neighbors we had come to know while doing this was having a cookout and invited us to join them for dinner. Of course, we accepted the offer and decided to remain running the radar trap until six thirty in the evening when dinner would be ready. It was a twenty-five-mile-per-hour zone in a very condensed residential area. Most of the violators were not more than ten miles per hour over the limit. Suddenly, we picked up this truck on radar, doing forty-five miles per hour, twenty miles per hour over the limit. He was pulled over, and before we could ask for his license and registration, he blurted out, "You're not supposed to be here now! I told the chief four to five thirty."

Guess who? The guy who led the petition to have us set up there so often. Needless to say, he did not get just a verbal or written warning. Although this was the most humorous, I saw numerous similar examples in my career where the biggest complainers were the biggest offenders. I encourage citizens to report areas where speeding is a problem, but make sure you are not part of the problem.

Excessive speeding is probably the most common complaint most police departments will receive. It is a legitimate complaint because the law of physics applies. Not even considering a driver's reaction time or variables relating to the vehicles equipment, a vehicle of a certain weight traveling at a certain speed under certain conditions will take a specific amount or space to come to a stop. Regardless of how good of a driver you are and how alert you are, when that child comes running out after a runaway ball, you are not going to be able to stop in time. Increased speed is also going to increase the amount of potential damage. You are going to get hurt a lot more when a car traveling fifty miles per hour hits you, compared with being hit by a car traveling twenty-five miles per hour. Both hurt, but you are more likely to survive the lower speed collision.

The solution to speeding complaints is traffic enforcement. It is not setting up a little flashing sign telling people how fast they are going. Another solution frequently implemented, which I believe does not work, is the installation of four-way stop signs. This usually happens when citizens contacts their elected local official. As a means to placate the constituent, a four-way stop sign is installed. This creates a situation where, eventually, all people will tend to ignore the slew of stop signs as they try to drive from point A to point B in their neighborhood. Stop signs are perfect for controlling traffic at intersections but should not be used for speed control. Maj. Wayne Gallagher was the one who pointed this out to me early in my career, and it proved truthful. As an alternative to this, you might want to suggest to the council person who wants to keep speed down in a specific neighborhood, "Stop trying to 'fix' all the speeding tickets being issued to your constituents who are the ones actually speeding in that neighborhood."

Your traffic division is also going to be responsible for accident reconstruction. As patrol officers right out of the police academy, we were expected to be able to create a diagram of an accident scene. Such documentation was such that at a later time, the accident could be recreated, placing all fixtures, controls, vehicles, and people where they were found at the time of the accident. As unbelievable as it may sound now, cameras were not readily available, so it was important to document all the pertinent data. As technology expanded, the ability to document and analyze accidents (crashes) became much more sophisticated. With these advancements, you need specially trained officers who are able to use and apply this technology.

Commercial-vehicle enforcement is another area where traffic officers need additional training and certification. Without getting into great detail, the laws relating to the operation of commercial vehicles are much more stringent and require officers who are familiar with these laws. At bare minimum, you need to have a resource you can reach out to for assistance in accidents involving commercial vehicles.

Many people wonder about the quota of tickets that an officer is required to write. Some places have written policies, while others have an unwritten expectation. We had an unwritten expectation of twenty violations a month. Now some of you are screaming, "I knew it!" but think it through. On an average month, an officer works twenty days. If they are properly doing their job, they should see at least one violation that warrants a violation a day. These violations did not have to be tickets with a fine. A written warning and a five-day notice to get a defective vehicle repaired are counted. I think this was a very lenient quota for officers to maintain. Does a day go by that you don't see a motor-vehicle violation that you feel to be excessive, just hoping that there is an officer right around the corner? It is a police officer's job to locate those problems, so I don't think finding one a day is excessive or unrealistic.

Your traffic division needs to be set up and operated as an investigative unit, supplemented by enforcement, which will allow your community to be safer. It should not become a cash cow looking for new ways to build the municipality's coffers. The latter is not going to be good for the quality of life in your community and will not foster good relations with your police department and the citizens.

CHAPTER

15

# DETECTIVE DIVISION

H aving had the privilege to work at the rank of detective and then later in my career as the detective commander allowed me great insight into this specialized field of policing.

In our department, the detective division consisted of various units: major crimes, financial crimes, juvenile, and BCI (Bureau of Criminal Identification), which most will recognize from TV as CSI—same thing, definitely a different budget).

I will say it again: all police officers should be investigators, but when you get assigned to a detective division, your focus needs to change. You need to focus on the type of crimes you have been assigned to solve. This is not the time to focus on illegally parked cars, noise complaints, dogs at large, etc. This is the time for you to focus on the crimes you have been assigned to solve, who is committing them, and identifying any crime patterns.

Hopefully, through your experience from years of working on the street in patrol, you have a good knowledge of who is likely to be committing these crimes and how to best apprehend them. It is also the time to hone those interview and interrogation skills as this is how you are most likely to solve the crimes you have been assigned to solve. The sooner the perpetrator is arrested and gotten off the street, the safer your community will be. Pro bono publico.

As I have said about appearance in patrol, I believe the same holds true in detectives. If you look as if you just got done with a game of dodge ball (maybe in some of our more community policing–oriented departments, you did) you are not going to get the same respect as an officer dressed appropriately. I am going to date myself here, but dress clothes make for a much more formal presentation than the casual look. You are not out looking to make buddies; you are out to present yourself as someone with authority. Why? Because you are representing authority. You have crimes to solve, and you need to at least look as if you can do it. Dressing professionally as if you mean business allows you to get on with your business. The first impression a victim, witness, or suspect has of you should NOT be whether or not you really are a police officer.

I have seen officers who have worked twenty-four hours straight on a major crime and still present authority and professionalism by their dress, albeit a little wrinkled and unkempt. The job of a detective is not easy. There are plenty of obstacles in your way to solving a crime that you have no control over; take care of the ones you have control over—your appearance, your mouth, and your listening skills.

The biggest factor in a successful investigation is your people skills. The principle of "one mouth, two ears" is a big factor in investigations. You are going to be interviewing people for much longer periods and often on repeated occasions. Your contact is going to be in a much more formal setting than when you are taking a report from someone on the road. You are hopefully building a relationship with the person you are interviewing or interrogating.

If it is a victim you are interviewing, you need to be compassionate and patient. You may not think what they have experienced is a big deal—for example, a stolen bike—but to them, it is upsetting. If they are the victim of a capital crime, they are likely to be devastated. Their first reaction might be "I already told the other officer what happened."

This is not the time to cop an attitude; this is the time to be patient and explain to them the need for retelling the story. This is the time to introduce yourself as the point person who will be responsible for investigating the case. You will likely need the cooperation of this victim to successfully investigate the crime. You want the victim to feel comfortable communicating with you. If the victim perceives that you are not looking out for their best interest, they are very likely to not be cooperative. If you are acting like a jerk, the victim may likely shut down and avoid you like a plague. Remember, you want to solve crime, not close cases because of uncooperative witnesses. Introduce your partners as soon as possible if other officers will be working the case with you. You want your victim and witness to be well informed and feel comfortable in providing you with information.

Your investigation most often starts with the interview, but there is a lot more to do. If possible, visit the crime scene. If it is an active crime scene, get permission to view it from the crime scene detectives on scene. With you wearing the proper apparel, most crime scene detectives will gladly show you around. This is a good way to observe the scene for yourself, and hopefully, you can make some deductions based on this. You can also determine if what your witness or victim told you is possible or probable. Review the evidence that has been identified already. Based on your interviews, there may be some additional evidence present that you feel should be secured. Relay this to the crime scene investigators. Your input and approval should be sought before any crime scene is released. You should have a good relationship with your crime scene investigators, and this should not be an issue. If there is a constant issue related to this, then your department needs to set up a policy to ensure that you as the lead detective have input on when a scene is released. This is so true in the case of a major crime. Frequently, as a result of interviews, investigators may want to secure additional evidence that was not initially evident from the crime scene. There should be no rush to release the scene as, once released, the challenge is on to introduce any subsequently seized evidence.

Continue the investigation. Talk to witnesses and possible witnesses, secure video from cameras surrounding the area, talk to informants, research data on the Internet, etc. Each investigation will be unique, and the investigative steps you take will vary, but the basic principle is investigate.

Document your investigative steps. This will help not only you but also those who are working alongside you. Again, I recommend you make a hard copy and use a notebook to record your investigation. At the end, you can enter all the data, nice-nice, into some form of central database, but paper and pen are your friend on the street. I know we live in the day of digital media, which I encourage, but the fact remains that all electronic devices and all electronic storage databases fail at some point. It can be a minor failure where the system is not available or a critical one where your entire database is corrupted. If you have relied on this system and don't have hard copies, the whole case is in trouble.

Once you have determined possible suspects, get them in for an interview. It's not television. If they are free to go and not under arrest, you don't have to Mirandize them at this point. (Check the latest court decision in your state as this may have changed.) If there is sufficient probable cause, arrest them. Now you can have your interrogation after they have received and signed the waiving of their Miranda rights. If they want a lawyer, get them one and then do your interrogation.

Once you start interviewing a suspect, this is the time for YOU to look for evidence on the suspect. Look for wounds that are consistent with someone who committed the crime. Look at the shoe patterns to see if they are similar to those prints left at the crime scene and personal effects that may contain information about the victim. Get a consent to search, or a search warrant, to see what is on their cellphone. This is the day and age where everyone loves to take pictures of everything they do, and criminals are certainly part of that trend. How many videos have you seen on the web of criminals documenting their crime? Lots. There is no limit on what evidence you may find just during the interview.

Even though all the evidence may be pointing to a certain suspect, even enough evidence to secure a warrant, be open-minded when you do your interview or interrogation. Possibly, the person you are interviewing may not be the suspect at all. Frequently, evidence is so overwhelming that the likelihood of someone else being responsible for the crime is not apparent. That is why it is important to begin your interview with an open mind. The science of interviewing and interrogating is one of those areas where there is a wide variety of courses and seminars available to you. I encourage you to further your education in interview and interrogation techniques. This will make you a better detective and help with your clearance rate.

When you are interviewing or interrogating a suspect, treat them with respect, regardless of the crime. Your goal in the interview or interrogation is to secure evidence and, hopefully, get a confession. This is not going to be achieved if you spend the first ten minutes of the interview telling the suspect what a lousy, dirty, filthy piece of trash they are. Even if those thoughts are running through your mind, be professional and conduct yourself as such.

One thing about interviewing a suspect—at the end of the interview, you should know more about the suspect than the suspect knows about you. I had the pleasure of working with one of our most decorated detectives and successful interrogators, Det. Cpl. Arthur Clark. This is one of the many insights he gave me into the investigative field: "This is not the time to tell someone how great thou art. Nor is this the time to reveal information about you as a person. Some slick criminal is going to love knowing that you coach youth soccer with your children on Saturday at such and such a field."

If possible, you should always have two officers conducting an interview, and it should be documented, hopefully, digitally. Any confession is going to come under great scrutiny, more so based on the severity of the crime, so this is the time to secure that evidence.

At the end of the investigation, it is your responsibility as the lead detective assigned to the case to put the case together. Don't take a pile of reports and evidence reports and dump them on someone else to put together for you. Not only do they not have the personal knowledge that you do of your case, but also, it's your job. After all, you should take pride of this work in your investigation. After reviewing the case in entirety, you may realize that there is some further information you need to secure. You need to gather all the reports, statements, evidence inventories, crime laboratory reports, photographs, and anything else related to the case and put them together in an organized fashion. Close your investigation with a narrative that will provide a synopsis of the case and a list of all the evidence related to it. This should be done in such a fashion as a prosecutor will have no problem presenting it to a judge or a jury.

There is a lot of responsibility placed on detectives to solve cases. Oftentimes both the public and your fellow officers in patrol are counting on you to solve a case by putting the final pieces of the puzzle together. Don't let them down because most often you are the one who will make or break a case.

Det. Lt. James Trail on his last day of duty

Detectives' golf tournament
Atty. Paul Daly, Det. Cpl. Arthur Clark, Myself, Det. Cpl. Stanley Chin

# CHAPTER 16

# VICE INVESTIGATIONS

When I first joined the police force, the vice squad focused mainly on illegal-drug investigations, gambling, and prostitution. Approximately 2 percent of the force was assigned to investigate these crimes. There was no Internet readily available to facilitate these criminal enterprises. In 1979, drugs were the main focus, and illegal gambling received the least attention. This is a good example of how common sense needs to be applied to law enforcement. There are just so many officers available, and if you go back to the basic tenant of protecting life and property, illegal drug activity definitely has the greatest negative impact on society. For the sake of clarification, vice will include all the above crimes, but for the most part, I am referring to how to investigate illegal drugs in the body of this chapter.

Once assigned to a vice or narcotics unit, your investigative techniques are the same as when you were a patrol officer or a worker in any other investigative unit. This, however, is the time for casual dress. Get out of the Power Ranger pajamas and have a blast. Give the razor and your face a break. Don't overdo it though. What does someone who buys and sells drugs look like? The average citizen. It could be Wall Street Wally in his suit, picking up some cocaine or selling cocaine to his suit buddies. It could be Big Eddy with his name tag on his commercial laundry shirt, getting off the second shift at the factory, looking for some pills. It could be Trixie Trailerpark looking like Trixie Trailerpark, out trying to score some heroine. They look like this and everything and everyone in between. The point is don't overdo the disguise. If you are "fashionably challenged," as Lt. Tommy Rush once accused me of being, don't go for the five-hundred-dollar tailored suit. Actually, when I was assigned undercover, my favorite go-to was a pair of blue farmer's jeans and the appropriate shirt and work boots. Chief Winquist was not happy at first. He told me that he was not going to reimburse me for them. (We had a clothing allowance in the unit.) However, as our unit's drug arrests started coming in, he got over the overalls, and yes, he reimbursed me.

I was fortunate enough to work in our vice unit for two years with Lt. Charles Hall, Capt. Joseph Broadmeadow, Capt. Walter Barlow, and Chief Kenneth Bilodeau. It was a great team, with just enough balance of personalities. The one thing about drug investigations is that for everyone you arrest, you create a new investigation. The goal is to go higher up the ladder to get to the real dealers who are making a fortune, don't use drugs themselves, and could care less about the carnage they are spreading in your community. But the reality of drug investigations is that you have to start somewhere, and that's usually at the bottom of the ladder—the users and street dealers out to support their own habit.

Narcotic investigations, like any other investigation, need to be documented. If there was ever a time not to have data loaded onto a database until an arrest is made, this is the time. I don't care how secure your system is; illegal drugs are big money, and the potential for corruption is high. Don't have data floating in the "cloud" for people to access.

Your communication skills are paramount. Know what you are talking about and what group you are talking to. The lingo for Wall Street Wally is not going to be the same as that for Big Eddy or Trixie Trailerpark. What is the street name of the drug? Often it could be simply the packaging type or size, with no mention of the actual product. The terms *eight-ball* and *bundle* never used the word *cocaine* or *heroin*, but all involved knew what you were referring to. Use lingo, nonverbal cues, etc., that your targets are familiar with. When it comes time for the interview after the arrest, then you need to put back on the hat of a professional investigator, not when you are out on the street.

Who should work undercover? Not the new officer. Using the new officer fresh out of the academy seemed to be the trend for many departments. Take someone right out of the academy and turn them loose in a world full of booze, drugs, sex, and criminals. Personally, I think this is a horrible choice as you have no real idea what the character of the new officer is. They have not learned what it is like to be a police officer. The world of an undercover officer is not the place to learn how to be a good police officer. If you feel that your officers cannot go undercover because they will be easily recognized, set up a mutual aid situation with another department. Their officers can go undercover in your city, and your officers can go undercover in theirs. It works well, and we did it all the time with other departments in our state.

"How do officers who have already had numerous contacts with drug dealers work in vice?" you might ask. Very well. My partners in the vice unit mentioned above along with myself served over eight years as patrol officers on the street before being assigned to the vice unit. Prior to this assignment, we were all very active officers, having had a lot of prior contact with the criminal element. Officers who are assigned to vice should be well-trained investigators with good street smarts. You can also run a very successful vice investigation by observing from afar, applying for search warrants, wiretaps, clone phones, or arrest warrants, without ever interacting with drug dealers face-to-face.

Informants are a big factor in vice investigations, and you don't need to be undercover to work with an informant.

How do you develop informants? Use your basic investigative skills. If someone is arrested by patrol for possession of drugs, go have a chat with them, especially if they have been sitting in jail all night. Street people know the street, even if they are not involved in that particular illegal activity themselves.

If they are willing to provide you with some information, work out a deal and move up that ladder. If the suspect agrees to work with you, don't make the mistake of letting someone go without holding the charge over their head. Set parameters, such as "If you do so and so, we will drop or reduce the charges against you."

Make sure you get approval for your recommendation before offering it from the proper authority, whether it is within the department or from the attorney general's office. And whatever you promised to do, if they have lived up to their end of the deal, DO IT. Don't promise something and then NOT fulfill your promise. Unfortunately, the latter happens a lot, and suspects will be leery about cooperating with you or any other officer in the future. If you get a reputation as being an officer of your word, you will earn respect. If you do not fulfill your promises, you'll get a reputation of being a liar. You will get nowhere in your investigations and will very likely have some resentful criminals looking for a chance to get back at you.

We had a case one time where a large amount of cash with drug residue on it was seized from a known drug dealer. We told the suspect that the money was going out to the lab for analysis, and if it came back positive for cocaine, we were getting a warrant for them. The suspect was offered the option of cooperating in lieu of charges should it test positive. The person was a very hard-core individual, well entrenched in the drug trade, so we didn't expect to see them again until such time as we had an arrest warrant. About two weeks went by, and this person came into the station and asked to see the money. We informed this person we were not giving it back at this point as we were still waiting to get the lab results back. The suspect said he just wanted to see it. We brought the suspect in and showed the bag with the money in it, marked with the crime lab's markings. The suspect's response was "You really did send it out for testing. I thought you were going to grab the money for yourselves. Now that I know that, I'll work with you."

Does the scorn of an ex-spouse ring any bells? This person provided so much information that after executing numerous search warrants ourselves, we had to forward some of the information onto state and federal agencies. This person was not the only one whom we had a similar experience with. Criminals need to know they can trust you and that you are honest.

How did this major drug dealer get arrested? Like many drug dealers who initially got arrested. Patrol officers were part of our information chain. It was a patrol officer who observed the suspect operating an unregistered car. Like any good patrol officer, he was not only focused on handing out a ticket and getting an unregistered car towed but also used his investigative skills during the routine traffic stop and subsequent vehicle inventory to find and seize contraband. He then made the appropriate documentation and notification to vice. Team effort. This is the type of officer you want to eventually put into a vice unit, not the new officer coming out of the academy.

Informants are a very integral part of vice investigations. You need to respect your informant, and they need to respect you. Make sure you establish what your guidelines are. Don't let an informant run amok. If someone is dealing drugs all day long and only gives you some tidbits on their competition, you are not solving the problem. You are actually making yourself and your department look foolish. If you tell your informant you are going to protect their identity, do it. Even if the case is going to get dismissed, keep your word. Again, there is too much money involved in the illegal drug trade to have someone murdered under your watch simply to get a conviction. There are not many but some dirty lawyers and judges who would have no problem pushing for the identity of the informant, simply to pass the information onto the suspect.

There are professional informants. When I first heard of this in the police academy, I didn't believe such a thing existed. But then as my career progressed, I realized they do exist. This can create a problem. You need to protect the informant's identity while providing accountability for the money you are spending on their "salary," in addition to the money you forward to these individuals to make purchases. For this purpose, we had a secure (paper) file with basic information locked in the chief's office. A number was assigned to each informant, and all accounting simply listed the informant's number. This is a nice check-and-balance system for any undercover operation to ensure the money is not being used improperly.

I personally feel that 80 to 90 percent of all crimes committed today can be traced back to illegal drug activity and substance abuse. I did not check any studies, and I don't know if any exist to prove or disprove my statement, nor do I care.

On a side note, I often found that many studies and statistics tend to have an underlying goal. The next time you hear a number tossed out, especially if it is followed by a solicitation, do some basic math and determine if it is probable or even possible.

I heard a quote one time. "Numbers are like people. If you torture them enough, they will tell you whatever you want."

An example of this that I experienced was back in 1984 when I was told that the supply of crude oil would be gone by 2004 and that it was vital to pay four thousand dollars to purchase solar panels so I would be able to heat my house. There was a large array of statistics and numbers presented during the two-hour presentation supporting this presumption. I assumed the facts and statistics were twisted, but I was promised a thirty-five-millimeter camera if I stayed for the whole presentation. My thought process going into this seminar was "How bad can a thirty-five-millimeter camera really be?"

I found out.

The negative impact of substance abuse affects all of us, regardless of socioeconomic level, race, religion, age, sex, sexual orientation, etc. During my career, I saw the drastic increase in the demand for illegal drugs. It is a societal problem that cannot simply be addressed by legislation.

Today we have some very high-ranking people, including legislatures and even some in law enforcement, promoting drug use. They want to legalize everything from marijuana to heroine. I simply cannot understand their rationale. They may be uneducated, cowards or, worse, greedy individuals seeking to make great profits at the cost of society's misery. I simply don't know what drives them to think this way, but I cannot, based on my years of experience, go along with this philosophy.

We always hear about the drug war. I honestly don't think we ever really started fighting it. One blunder years ago was Washington DC's answer to the cocaine problem. In the District of Columbia, mandatory jail for anyone caught with "crack" cocaine became the law. It did nothing but crowd jails, take the focus away from dealers, and provide no long-term rehabilitation for those arrested. Throughout the country, we have lots of laws relating to illegal drugs, but very few provide for a real deterrent to drug dealers, and most importantly, very little effort is put into rehabilitation. Instead of prison, so many people addicted to drugs could certainly benefit from a long-term treatment plan that is isolated from society. This includes family, friends, and phones. Allow these people to be free from addiction. Yes, drug withdrawal is not a pleasant situation, but once done, these people could start putting their lives back together. These weekend retreats or government-financed replacement drugs, such as methadone, do nothing to eliminate the addiction but certainly make some people very rich.

If you are a vice investigator, stay informed of the current trends and pass this information onto those officers working the streets. If you are an officer working the street, pass this information onto vice as they may not be aware of it. Street knowledge is vital. Dating myself, the surge of cocaine started while I was a patrol officer. There was not a lot of information available to us at the time. Marijuana, pills, and heroine were the most common illegal drugs we would encounter on the street. Using the "common sense" principle, on many occasions, we would seize a small quantity of marijuana. We would have a little chat with the suspect and destroy it on the spot in their presence. Almost always, the people we seized it from were very grateful and often provided intelligence at a later date. It also fostered a bit of respect between both parties. I am not sure this lack of information was always healthy for the suspect. It was at this period when we were first learning about cocaine (packaging, value, paraphernalia, etc.) that Cpl. Dick Szleiga and I stopped a car coming from Cape Cod. The guy had a kilo of cocaine in his possession, about the same size as a couple of pounds of marijuana. It was an extremely busy night, and suddenly, a call came in for shots fired. Prioritizing our responsibility, we told the guy it was his lucky day. We cut open the kilo of cocaine, tossed it into a busy four-lane highway, and watched as numerous vehicles disintegrated it. The guy stood there in a state of shock as we told him to drive away. We didn't understand his reaction until later when we talked to the vice detectives. We learned that a kilo of cocaine at the time cost quite a bit more than a pillow of marijuana.

When working in vice, you need to work with other agencies. Know who your counterparts are throughout your region and get to know them on a personal level. Like any other crime and much more so with narcotics, people are crossing municipal boundaries. If you don't establish relationships with your counterparts, your work is going to be much harder. We were blessed to have relationships with other investigators, not only from other local municipalities but also from state and federal agents as well. We had contacts within the FBI, DEA, ATF, Secret Service, and Immigration (now ICE). When I say *contacts*, I am not referring to someone you could just contact on the phone; I am referring to contacts in the sense that you would meet and work with one another on a regular basis. In spite of all you may read or hear, the federal agents we knew from these agencies were always willing to help. There were no jurisdictional turf wars as you so often see on television. I was amazed at the cooperation we received from these agents, even for small local investigations. If we needed extra bodies for a drug raid at the local bar, we wouldn't think twice about asking some of these agents, even though there were no federal crimes committed. It was a two-way street. If they needed help, we were always there to assist. You felt very comfortable passing information onto them as you knew they would respect the confidentiality and actually do something with the information you gave them besides enter it into a database.

Vice investigations are going to be time-consuming and will require well-vetted, dedicated officers to conduct these investigations. Because drugs are placing such a burden on our society, this is an area where your department needs to focus. Please don't think your community is exempt from this plague.

My undercover days with "Sergeant Slaughter" and
Armen Garo at the Special Olympics

CHAPTER

17

# CRIME SCENE INVESTIGATIONS

A crime scene investigation will probably be most familiar to people through the numerous shows on television where a group of officers will arrive at a major crime scene, photograph it, search for and gather evidence, and then process it in their million-dollar laboratory, comparing the results with every human being on the planet. While all crime scene investigators would love to have that technology and that budget, the reality is it does not exist for the most part in the real world. Also, most crime scenes that need to be processed are not major crimes. This chapter is not going to explain how a gas chromatograph can identify a material found in the suspect's shoes and connect it to a specific location. It is going to deal with the basics of policing and what you should do as an officer, what you should provide as an administrator, and what the public should reasonably expect from their police department.

Crime scene investigators are looking for forensic evidence. An early pioneer of forensic science, Dr. Edmond Locard developed the Locard's exchange principle. This principle holds that every perpetrator of a crime will bring something into the crime scene and leave with something from it. "Every contact leaves a trace." This was summed up nicely by Paul L. Kirk's statement in the book *Crime Investigation: Physical Evidence and the Police Laboratory*, Interscience Publishers Inc., New York (1953).

> Wherever he steps, whatever he touches, whatever he leaves, even unconsciously, will serve as a silent witness against him. Not only his fingerprints or his footprints, but his hair, the fibers from his clothes, the glass he

breaks, the tool mark he leaves, the paint he scratches, the blood or semen he deposits or collects. All of these and more, bear mute witness against him. This is evidence that does not forget. It is not confused by the excitement of the moment. It is not absent because human witnesses are. It is factual evidence. Physical evidence cannot be wrong, it cannot perjure itself, it cannot be wholly absent. Only human failure to find it, study and understand it, can diminish its value.

The above quote is courtesy of Wikipedia (2017).

As with most aspects of police work, the patrol officers working on the street are almost always going to be the ones who come upon a crime scene first. Oftentimes they are going to be the ones securing and seizing evidence. It is vital to have all your officers well trained in crime scene preservation and evidence collection. This should be done in the academy, but to make sure, you need to set up policies, guidelines, and training before they ever get onto the street by themselves.

There should be officers assigned to a specialized crime scene investigation unit, but all officers should be well versed in evidence collection and preservation. I was fortunate to have spent two years working in BCI (Bureau of Criminal Investigation) as an investigator. Lt. James Trail was my mentor and guided me through this period of my career. Fortunately, later on in our career, we both worked together again, only this time, as supervisors of this same unit. Fortunately for those working in the unit at the time, we realized its importance and increased the staffing while providing them with the tools they needed. Unfortunately, for those working in the unit at the time, the excuse of "we can't get evidence from this because . . ." didn't fly well with either of us because we both knew better. There was always one time we could predict a major crime occurring. Because of our experience and the fact all the officers assigned to that unit wanted to have a yearly getaway retreat together, we would offer to cover for those days. In six years, I don't remember one time when one of us didn't have to put on our BCI hat and process a major scene. I had no regrets. It kept us sharp and allowed the officers to build on their camaraderie.

The success of your crime scene investigation unit is related to training. Officers assigned to that unit need to get specialized training in forensics, and they should be encouraged to continue with their college education and take classes that will assist them in the field of forensics, such as chemistry, microbiology, electronics. What is going to complement this unit is to make sure that your patrol officers are well trained. Our department constantly trained our patrol officers through in-service seminars and hands-on training. This training also extended to our evidence eradication unit, also known as the fire department. I say this in jest as a fire fighter's mission is much different than that a crime scene investigator. Their primary focus is on saving lives, not evidence preservation. Joint training allows for your fire fighters to be aware of evidence preservation while performing their duties. Based on years of joint training, our fire fighters were very alert and cooperative in this aspect.

Most crime scenes are not going to involve a major crime, and patrol officers are going to be the ones identifying and securing evidence. To assist them with this, we instituted a policy where all patrol vehicles had an evidence-collection kit. This allowed officers the tools they needed to secure evidence from minor crime scenes. They were very basic kits. I have included the contents of the memorandum at the end of this chapter should you want to use it for ideas.(1) It had enough equipment for officers to properly secure evidence from a crime scene as well as secure a crime scene. With the technology today, almost everyone has a cell phone with a camera. This was not always the case, and our department was one of the first to get cameras out in the field with supervisors. Back then, a good thirty-five-millimeter camera was an expense. Today it is not so much of an expense; however, the use of cell phone cameras presents many issues. You need a policy dealing with the use of personal cell phones to record criminal evidence. If officer use their cellphones to take a photograph, their cellphone in entirety could end up being turned over to the defense for evidence. I don't think any of us want our personal information in the hands of anyone. I assume that many officers would be more than willing to use their personal cell phone cameras to record crime scenes. They are eager to solve crimes, and this is a tool at their disposal. Administrators, you need to protect your officers. A decent digital camera is very economical today. Buy enough so your patrol officers have access to them. I know my department recently implemented a policy where every patrol car assigned to a beat has a digital camera. If your department has done the right thing and provided you with a camera to use, don't use your cell phone camera and then post work-related photos on social media. There are good defense lawyers out there who have personnel perusing the Internet for just such material. Not only is all the personal data on your cell phone going to the defendant and who knows who else, but also the question of withholding evidence may come up, and your criminal case could start having "reasonable doubts." Remember, common sense.

As a crime scene investigator, your first job at a scene should be to speak with the patrol officers who were the first on scene. Oftentimes there will be some time delay before you get there, and they should have some great insight. One case I vividly remember when I was working in patrol with Lieutenant Ezovski was a sudden death call we went to. It was an elderly lady who had passed, apparently from one of the multiple illnesses she was suffering. It seemed to be a death because of natural causes. We did a visual check of the body and the room, and nothing seemed suspicious. It was not until we had spent about an hour, waiting for the medical examiner, with the husband that we started having second thoughts about the cause. His wife had been deceased for less than an hour, and we could not help but notice how quickly he was starting to clear things out of the house. Nothing from the bedroom where the victim lay but books, knickknacks, etc. He was not only actively throwing them into garbage containers but also talking out loud to himself about how he could "finally get rid of this ——." After about an hour of this, he approached us and asked us, "Is there any way you guys can toss her in your trunk and drive her to the Cape? She always wanted to be buried there."

After we told him no, we both took a second look around to see if there were any noticeable indications of foul play we may have missed at first. When the medical examiner finally arrived, we relayed these observations to him. It turned out the death was from natural causes, and this was one of the most bizarre grieving mechanisms I had ever seen, but it shows that you not only need to observe but also continue to observe and communicate, either orally or in written form, what you observe.

When you are collecting evidence, be aware of the Fourth Amendment. It is the legal precedence to conduct the search and make a seizure or do you need to get a search warrant? Know and be able to explain the rationale of exigent circumstances. Oftentimes with a serious crime, the suspect can easily eliminate culpable evidence from their person. This is the time to keep them handcuffed behind their back to prevent them from secreting or destroying any evidence that may be on them. Be alert to this, and start securing the evidence as soon as practical. We had a nice collection of clothing, courtesy of our local secondhand store, which we could provide the suspects once we seized their clothes. Again, one of those common-sense things. Don't remove a suspect's clothes and have no other plans. The courts are not going to look kindly on you leaving someone naked simply because you needed to secure possible evidence. Evidence that is not going to be easily destroyed such as the suspect's DNA, blood type, and bite impression should only be obtained after getting a consent to search or a search warrant.

When searching a building, vehicle, etc., again, a consent to search, or a search warrant, should be secured when practical. If evidence is being destroyed in your presence, then obviously, exigent circumstances exist. If you are questioning yourself if you need a search warrant, get advice from a supervisor but err on the side of caution. Search warrants can be time-consuming, but the time is certainly well spent if it is going to allow you to enter all the evidence you have seized in a court of law.

Your crime scene needs to be secured as you only get one shot at the evidence. Once a scene is released, people are free to come and go into it, and any subsequent evidence seized is going to be tainted, and you are going to have great difficulty entering it as evidence in a court of law.

Securing the crime scene is vital. One of the first things you need to set up—again, most likely, the patrol officer who was first at the scene—is a crime scene log. Document who goes in, what date and time, and when they leave. Depending on the nature of the scene, you are going to need to mark it off. Crime scene tape is the most basic way to do this. Only those people who are going to be a part of the investigation should be in the crime scene. This primarily includes the crime scene investigators. The crime scene investigator should be delegated the ultimate authority and responsibility on who is allowed into the scene. At this moment in time, they should outrank everyone. Once secured, the detectives actually working the case should be allowed inside once they are properly gowned and gloved. This allows the investigator to get a firsthand look on what happened. I don't remember who taught me this principle, possibly Capt. Joseph Crevier who was the BCI expert when I got on the job, but an ideal thing to do is set up a secondary perimeter. This is where all the people who think they are important can go and stand around. It provides for an area where they can be set apart from the crowd while preserving the actual crime scene.

Crime scene investigators need the proper equipment to process a crime scene. This is not the area you want to look at when you do budget cuts. What I believe to be most important is a suitable vehicle. When I first got on the job, the government was supplying BCI vans to police departments through grants, which were specifically designed for average departments to have a means of securing evidence. We used this van for years, including the time I was assigned there. When this finally had to be put out of service, someone had a bright idea of using a Ford Taurus that was used for a few years. This is not a good vehicle for the purpose of carrying all the equipment needed for crime scene investigation. When Lieutenant Trail and I first took over the detective division, I remember our plan was to use an old rescue vehicle from the fire department to be used for crime scene investigations. We had a conversation with then City Manager Lemont. He was concerned that once we instituted an old rescue vehicle, we then would have to provide for a new one when it was put out of service. We told him that we won't need a new one, but we would always need a similar vehicle. Because of the fact the fire department would always have used rescues available, there would not be any issues. Now if your municipality has the budget, go for the brand-new crime scene vehicle. There are some top-of-the-line models out there with all the bells and whistles. If you get one of these high-end models, use it. Don't let it sit for months, and then when you actually need it, it won't start. Get input from the crime scene officers doing the job and find out what they need. If the cost is reasonable, have faith in your officer's judgements and get it. Don't listen to some salesperson and their recommendations. A department working in a beach community is going to need equipment much different than those departments working in Alaska. At bare minimum, you need a TRUCK with multiple compartments, thoroughly equipped, with the ability to generate electricity and provide for lighting at a crime scene.

Although DNA. analysis has become a great tool in identifying and connecting criminals to crime scenes, the time-proven technique of fingerprints is still more accurate. Identical twins will share the same genotype compared with fraternal twins, yet they will have different fingerprints. The science of fingerprints is a specialized field, but all officers should have a basic understanding of the science and how to identify, develop, and collect them. Again, technology has given us great tools to advance this process, most notably the AFIS system. We were fortunate to be one of the first departments in the state to get one of these systems. After our crime scene investigators became familiar with its operation, a training program was instituted to train all officers in securing fingerprints from suspects using the AFIS.

Fingerprints are often found at crimes scenes. Sometimes they are visible, but often they are latent. Latent fingerprints are not visible to the naked eye and require scientific processing to make them visible. Developing and preserving fingerprints at a crime scene is a very tedious and most often very messy task. Fingerprints have great evidentiary value, but you need to be able to compare them with something. You need to have a good fingerprint file within your department. There are automated systems to store these, but again, I would recommend keeping the hard file as well. The more fingerprints you can legally obtain from suspects, the better your database will be. Our policy involved fingerprinting every adult who was arrested and charged with a misdemeanor or a felony. We also fingerprinted juveniles for felony arrests yet kept the files separate. You need to confirm your policy against your state's criminal codes as they vary from state to state.

During my career, I had the honor of visiting Scotland Yard. Part of the tour included the fingerprint department, which was huge. The one thing I took away from this tour was the fact they secured palm prints from all the suspects they arrested. Having worked in the field, I realized how many times we found latent prints at a crime scene yet were unable to match them because they were not prints from the fingers. Often we would get palm prints from a suspect when in custody and suspected of a specific crime, but there was no policy requiring they were always taken. Shortly after this trip, we instituted a policy where palm prints were taken from everyone arrested for a felony. This was a great asset, and I encourage your department to institute a similar policy if one does not exist.

Police departments frequently take fingerprints from noncriminals for employment purposes, most notably those working with children. These need to be kept apart and returned to the applicant as soon as the background check is done. It may be tempting to keep them for your file, but you need to keep to the letter of the law and not bring a cloud or a lawsuit upon your agency.

Most police departments are going to depend upon a variety of laboratories dedicated to forensic science. These labs will usually be run by the state or county, but there is also the FBI crime lab used by most police departments. In my opinion, these outside agencies need good oversight, and I am not sure there always is. Police administrators need to be active in whatever oversight committee is in place for these labs. Investigators need to be alert to what is transpiring once evidence is transferred to these labs. Is it being processed in a timely manner? Are you constantly getting reports that are inconclusive? If so, start investigating. One time, we had a string of bank robberies. Captain Barlow was the lead investigator, and

I was working as a crime scene investigator. On the counter, Captain Barlow observed a visible shoe impression. Upon further examination, we observed a decent amount of broken glass within the impression. This was photographed and seized. Sometime later, when the suspects were identified, a search warrant was obtained for the suspect's house. During this search, a pair of shoes were recovered. Imbedded in the soles of the shoes with the same sole pattern as those found at the scene was glass, consistent with that found on the bank counter. We could visibly compare it and piece it together as a puzzle, but we chose to send it to the FBI crime lab in Washington DC. A conviction of the suspect was secured prior to the results coming back. Months later, we received the report from the FBI crime lab "inconclusive results."

From that moment on, the reputation of this lab was in question for most of us. Over the years, there have been many cases where a laboratory or medical examiner's office, which law enforcement greatly depends upon, have had various failures, which resulted in the reversal of many criminal convictions. Sometimes the number of reversals are in the thousands as was the case in Massachusetts in 2017. There is not a lot that can be done about this in hindsight, but you as the consumer and taxpayer need to keep abreast of how these agencies are performing. These agencies are usually out of the limelight, and without strong oversight, the potential for problems because of the lack of accountability increases.

The one constant related to crime is that there is always going to be physical evidence related to that crime. How well your department is able to identify, process, and connect that evidence to a criminal well impact how well your agency functions as a law enforcement agency.

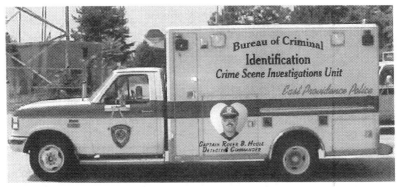

A mock design of our new BCI van.
Courtesy of the "free press"

(1) The evidence collection kit we used originated with patrol memorandum 95-9 and was incorporated into the department's rule and regulations. The kit consisted of the following items:

1. Paper bags, plastic bags, envelopes in assorted sizes
2. Needle boxes to protect law enforcement personnel from puncture wounds (a very common threat)
3. Rubber gloves
4. Marking crayons (don't be the chalk monster at a crime scene)
5. Evidence tags and elastics
6. Hemostats (usually courtesy of the vice squad destroying evidence)
7. Razor knifes
8. Crime scene tape
9. Styrene for securing sharp objects (not those with possible trace evidence)
10. Crime scene sign in sheet
11. Major crime scene checklist
12. Clear tape (ideal for securing powdery substances if they have been dumped out)

CHAPTER

18

# SUPERVISION

# PROMOTIONAL EXAMINATIONS

M ost all law enforcement agencies will have various ranks within the agency. As a rule, it will start with a patrol officer and progress to corporal, sergeant, lieutenant, captain, major (deputy chief), and finally, chief (colonel). As a rule, there is a requirement to move up the ranks consecutively. In my department, there was a minimum number of years served in a specific rank before being eligible for the next rank. The higher up you go, the more the criteria for a qualified candidate will change. There are exceptions, such as our department allowed a lieutenant with sufficient time in rank to be eligible to become the police chief. Now those from my era on the department who read this will immediately have a name pop up in their head.

Promotions should be made based on some objective criteria. The best way to test for this criterion is to have an independent written examination, an in-person review by a board, and then finally, an input from the officer's command staff. This input should be based not on popularity but on objective facts. These facts can include but are not limited to arrests, type of arrests, percent of investigations solved, sick use, disciplinary actions, and commendations.

I think it is important to make the examination material relevant to the job. Questions should be specific to your department and geographical area. A police department in a large urban area in the northeast is not likely to confront the same situations as they would in a small town in the southwest.

If it cannot be included in the written examination and for the cost municipalities pay for these exams it should be, you should include questions that are related to state and local laws in your oral review. Most oral interviews conducted in Rhode Island were done by officers of an equal or higher rank for the rank applied for from outside departments. This allowed for an objective review of the candidate. This is one of those points where interdepartmental assistance is valuable. I had the pleasure of sitting on a few of these oral interviews for other departments. The one thing I always did prior to the interview was to get a copy of the department's policies and procedures. I would look for one of the more outdated, practically unachievable ones and then ask the candidates how they planned on implementing it should they get the promotion. To be fair, most officers don't know all the policies from memory, so I handed out a copy of the specific policy prior to asking the question. This was not designed to trick anyone but to see how good their problem-solving skills were, along with their level of common sense.

One such question that I asked that comes to mind is when I sat on an oral board for the rank of lieutenant for a large city with a force of approximately two hundred officers. This meant they had dozens of officers on the street at one time with only one lieutenant. The policy clearly stated, "The officer in charge (lieutenant for this department) must be PRESENT during all interviews and interrogations."

Now if you have any knowledge of police work and what an officer in charge is responsible for, this is clearly a policy that cannot be adhered to. It was a pleasure to listen to the responses from six candidates. They all professionally explained that they understood the spirit of the policy but that it was not practical to fulfill it to the letter and then went on to explain how they would go about fulfilling their obligations, primarily through delegation of authority, while acknowledging their own vicarious responsibility. Based on their nonverbal reactions as they read through the policy and their opening response to the question, all six immediately picked up on the impracticality of fulfilling the policy. It was a pleasure to listen to the six of them, and then came number seven. Obviously, by the remarks from the chief who was also sitting on the panel, this was the "golden child." When I posed this question, I was stunned at the response. This lieutenant candidate repeatedly declared how they would uphold this policy to the letter. When asked for a further explanation, the same response came out. When I and others on the panel pointed to examples of it being impractical and, at times, impossible, such as a witness of an assault being interviewed by an officer at a hospital while the suspect in this assault is being interviewed by another officer at the police station. The same response was stated.

"I will make sure that I am present at all interviews."

No explanation on how that would be done, considering it is physically impossible to be in two places at once. I brought up a few other scenarios that defied the laws of science but to no avail. This was a perfect example of someone who is not going to be a good supervisor. Supervisors, like all officers, need to be able to adapt to unique situations quickly, thinking outside of the box and using good common sense.

Although most departments in Rhode Island used an objective testing procedure for promotions, there are still some who don't. What the trend is nationally, I don't know.

If your department does not have an independent examination process in place for promotions, you might want to start asking your elected officials why one does not exist. This is a key into having a solid law enforcement agency. Without solid leadership, there will most likely be chronic problems within an agency.

# CHAPTER 19

# SUPERVISION

# THE BASIC PHILOSOPHY

This is that step on the promotional ladder where you learn all about vicarious liability. You **ARE** responsible **FOR** the people working under you. You are also responsible **TO** the people working under you. Knowing that, you need to learn to be a supervisor, not a superior. Your rank may be a superior rank to those below you, but that should be the only thing superior. A good biblical principle is that which Jesus Christ taught—be a good servant. The more responsibility bestowed upon you, the greater a servant you need to become. Promotion to a supervisory rank is also a good time to remember the principle: "Don't forget where you came from." Let me repeat that—"Don't forget where you came from."

One of our officers who was allegedly one of the artists for the department's "free press" created a great cartoon relating to this topic.

I don't know if you have a "free press" within your department, but we certainly did. For the most part, it had proper boundaries, and it certainly provided for some comic relief. My head was frequently photoshopped onto the body of the pope, even though I am not a Catholic. It was also a great tool to provide peer pressure for those people not doing their optimal job as well as a means of administering a dose of humble pie when needed.

Back to the topic of "don't forget where you came from," regardless of who the artist was, the cartoon was titled the "Presto-Chango Sergeant Machine." One of the components on this assembly line machine, going from patrolman to sergeant, was a large bottle of "forget where you came from" juice being injected into the new supervisors. Enough said on this topic.

The first step in supervising is to know what the job task is for those whom you are responsible for. If you don't at least have a basic idea, you are going to have trouble helping them and supporting them in doing their job.

Another problem many supervisors face is they were not the poster child patrol officer. You may be *given* the rank, but you are going to need to *earn* the respect of your officers. Quite simply, if you were a "screw-up" as a patrol officer, then getting promoted and then expecting everyone under your command to do everything you *did not do,* you might be in for a surprise. That does not mean that you should do nothing; it means you need to start setting an example and gradually encourage the officers under your command to follow suit. So this is the part you should consider before you make rank while you are still working as a patrol officer. Everyone will remember if you were a "screw-up," and it will be a lot easier to be a good supervisor if you were not a "screw-up" to begin with.

Some basic principles for being a good supervisor are the following:

1. "Actions speak louder than words." Do yourself what you want and expect the officers in your command to do.

2. "Do as I do" should be the guidepost, not "Do as I say, not as I do." You need to set a good example to earn the respect of the officers you are responsible for.

3. "Be a leader." To lead, you need to be out in front. This does not mean you need to nor should you go to every call, but you need to have a working knowledge of what is going on with the officers under your command and intervene before a problem occurs. Don't go hide under your desk while a problem is underway, anticipating how you will deflect it from you. Guess what, vicarious liability does not care if you were under the desk or not and does not care how good your rationalization of how you were not responsible is. Take the lead and get out in front of controversial situations involving the officers under your command.

4. "Be the stop point of the downhill flow." If something goes wrong, don't immediately look to pass the problem down to one of your officers. Take responsibility and afford your officers the same consideration we give every criminal—innocent until proven guilty. That does not mean that you blindly cover illegal or improper acts; it means you allow for an investigation before you start pandering to the mob. Do twice as much listening as you do talking at this point of an incident. Don't say something to

the mob just because you know it will appease them at the time. Remember, sometimes the mob is looking to deflect attention away from the guilty as a means of protecting them or their own criminal activity. Putting the police and their perceived misconduct in the spotlight instead of the crime at hand is a great tool of distraction frequently used.

5.  "Learn to become a good servant." It may be tough term to swallow, but if you don't provide for the logistical and emotional needs of the officers under your command, they are not going to make it, you are not going to make it, and your community will not make it.

6.  "A chain is as strong as its weakest link." You need to make sure all the links are strong. This goes for those officers above you in command. It is easy to pick apart your leaders, but this only weakens the chain. Try to encourage them and build them up rather than tear them down. It is very easy to Monday morning quarterback people, but it is very destructive. It is much harder to take the weakest link and work on making them the best they can be. The long-term success will be worth your work. I once heard at a staff meeting from a cohort that he would like to be able to handpick the officers who worked for him. I reminded him that officers such as he described further would not need a supervisor, and he would be out of a job. A major part of your job as a supervisor is training, positive correction, character build-up, and quality of the officers who work for you.

Each level of supervisory rank will have a different mission. It is your job to identify your role in the chain of command and be the best you can be for that rank. Remember what it was like at the rank below you and learn the rank above you. I am very thankful for Lt. Richard Silva, Capt. David Allsworth, Capt. Doug McLaughlin, and Capt. William Benson when they were shift lieutenants for all the teaching they gave us in regard to this. Their rationale behind doing so may have been a little different, but in the end, they encouraged us to learn the responsibilities of the higher ranks, even when we were just patrol officers. This education proved instrumental in helping us all as we moved on in our careers. As you progress up the chain of command, always be that teacher. Be a good servant.

Once you attain a rank, you need to seek the advice of not only your peers but also the officers below your rank. You may have accidentally ingested some "forget where you came from" juice and need to eat a little "humble pie" to counteract its effects. This is particularly important when you are at the top, and your source of advisors is limited. This happens often during night shifts when the administrators are not present. They are getting their rest and enjoying personal life while the final decision on major situations rests on your shoulders. I was in this position often as the midnight lieutenant. I and ten other people, including the two dispatchers, were responsible for maintaining law and order in a city of fifty thousand people. I am grateful to the advice I received from the sergeants and others who were working with me. Most of the time on these shifts, I was seeking the advice of my two sergeants at the time, Lt. Stephen Kennedy and Sgt. John Burney. These officers gave great insight and provided for an alternative point of view, and I am very thankful for their input. Just because the administration may not be working does not mean they should not be notified when a major crisis happens. In fact, they should be notified, and a system should be in place to ensure these notifications are made in a timely manner.

Supervision will be covered further in this book, but if you don't have a solid framework established on how supervisors are selected and how they are expected to perform, you need to implement one as without it, your department will be suffering a basic element it desperately needs.

# SUPERVISION

# DISCIPLINE

D iscipline is needed in any organization, and law enforcement is no exception. Law enforcement officers are working in the "fishbowl." Their actions are in public view most of the time, and therefore, any mistakes they make come under a lot of scrutiny.

As with all discipline administered in life, each incident that occurs in a law enforcement agency needs to be fully examined, and then the discipline should be appropriate to the situation. When I state "fully examined," I mean you need to look at all the circumstances surrounding the infraction.

Although rare, and I emphasize *rare*, there are some officers who use their authority as a law enforcement officer to operate as a criminal. Some unfortunately take a dark turn after they have been hired and start doing this. Others join the force, already being a member of a criminal organization, with the sole intent of furthering the interests of the criminal organization they belong to. When these individuals are caught and there is sufficient evidence, they deserve to be punished in accordance with the law. I believe in supporting police officers, but these people are not only criminals but also a disgrace to law enforcement.

With the exception already covered above, I will address the normal infractions that may occur within a law enforcement agency. First, you must realize that discipline needs to be corrective, not punitive. Infractions cover a wide spectrum of severity. If criminal activity is not involved, what is the best way to handle these as a supervisor? The first question to ask yourself is "Did I ever do this same thing and, by the grace of God, did not get caught?"

Or consider what you would do if your closest partner on the job committed this same infraction. How will your disciplinary actions affect the overall morale of your department?

Based on the circumstances, some infractions should just be ignored. Assume your department has a policy that officers will wear uniform hats whenever they are outside of the car. As a supervisor, you drive into a lot at three in the morning, and you observe an officer outside of the car, proactively checking a building for criminal activity, not wearing a hat. Personally, I would say nothing, let alone discipline verbally, and I definitely would not advise initiating formal discipline. If it were three in the afternoon and you observed an officer walking around with the public without a hat, I would say a verbal discussion is warranted.

Ask yourself how many infractions you committed before you got to work today. Did you use your directional all the time? Did you adhere exactly to the speed limit? Did you send a text on your phone? When you ran into the store for a quick item, did you park in a restricted area? We all break the letter of the law every day. Common sense needs to apply to life, and the law enforcement profession is no different.

There needs to be a policy to address internal-affair problems within every police department. In smaller departments, it could be supervisors assigned to this task. In larger departments, there will be an internal affairs office that reports directly to the top administrators. Now sometimes in our kinder and gentler world, we now call this the office of professional standards. It sounds a little softer but, I think, pretty lame. Every police officer gets the gist of what "internal affairs" stands for. I'm not sure if the other term carries the same clout. Those officers who are assigned to internal affairs need to have a very unique personality. You need to be fair, have good common sense, have great investigative skills proven by your actions on the job, and have tough skin. This is not the place to make new friends, nor should it be. It is one of the necessary evils that is part of law enforcement, and you as an officer need to respect the need for such a unit to exist.

The internal affairs unit should have a standardized procedure that all officers are aware of. Complaints should be handled initially, confidentially, and thoroughly. As I have discussed already, a complete investigation is needed before any action is recommended. Remember, your actions as an internal affairs officer can have a great impact on an officer's career, and before you make any formal allegations that would negatively impact that career, you need to be sure the action you are taking is warranted and will result in the proper correction of a situation. If your investigation is such that it exonerates an officer from allegations made against them, then your reported decision needs to be able to withstand judicial review.

Internal investigations and discipline will also be affected by various laws that exist in your state, which I will discuss under "police unions." If you are assigned to internal affairs, know what these laws are so that you do a service to all involved.

# SUPERVISION

# MAKE A DECISION AND ACT ON IT

There should be no need of this chapter, but having experienced the negative impact of nondecisiveness, I chose to include it. You cannot afford to be indecisive as a police officer. This is especially true if you are a police supervisor. You also cannot always be politically correct as a supervisor. You need to have compassion and a sense of justice, but you need to be able to act and make decisions. There are only two choices—the right decision and the wrong decision. If you make the right decision, you can move on. If you make the wrong decision, you can acknowledge the fact it was wrong, adapt, and modify it until you make it the right decision. People respect wrong decisions when they are made with good intentions. People do not respect someone making no decision at all. It presents weakness and a lack of self-confidence, and most importantly, if an issue is not addressed, the problem persists and often gets worse.

Once a decision is made, act on it. Capt. Dennis Charbonneau once blurted out a great statement while in the middle of a mix up during my daughter's funeral: "A FOULED-up decision well executed is better than a good decision which is never executed." He may not have used the word *fouled*, but I hope you get the idea.

At one point in my career, I noticed that one of my coworkers, Cpl. Fred George, who was the complete opposite of my conservative point of view, would often adjust his schedule to work with me when I was the road sergeant. One day, I asked him why he chose to work with me so often. His response was heartwarming: "Roger, I don't agree with most of your views, but I know when I am working with you, you are going to make a decision, and we are going to be moving like a runaway freight train."

That is the type of statement that supervisors like to hear. This is part of that building-up process that goes both ways in the chain of command. If a supervisor makes a decision that makes your life easier or is the right thing to do, thank them. On the same note, when the officers under your command perform well, commend them. There is nothing wrong with walking into roll call and publicly commending officers who did a great job on something.

How do you make decisions as a law enforcement supervisor? You make them the same way you would with the rest of your life, but now you have to factor in many more factors. You have to consider how your decision affects the citizens you are sworn to protect and how your decision affects the officers working under your command as well as those above you. You need to consider what impact your decision will have on the civil rights of the people you are directly dealing with. You need to consider all these factors into your decision and then make a decision in a timely manner to preserve life and property. One more thing to add to your decision-making process is the fact that whatever you decide, many people will be reviewing your decision for years to come. Is it difficult sometimes to make a good decision? Yes. Are you always going to make the right decision? No. Is it imperative that as a supervisor, you make a decision? YES.

The more educated you are in your profession as a police officer, the easier your decision-making process will be for you. Your professional police reports documenting your decision will also make the review a lot easier as well.

The basic guidepost for all your decisions is to remember that your mission is to protect life and property and to maintain order.

# ADMINISTRATION

This is that point in your career where you are commanding a division, serving as a chief or deputy chief or as a public safety director. This is also where some underqualified or unqualified people take on a role that they are not trained for nor are they ready for. If you are appointed as an administrator, you are still a supervisor, not the supreme dictator, so take all your supervisory skills with you and use them.

As a citizen, what is your municipality's hiring practices for these jobs? If it does not focus on a qualified officer's coming-up through the ranks, then you have some issues at hand. If the talk is that there are no qualified officers available, then you have some real issues at hand, and you need to put the spotlight on your elected officials. Short of a horrific disaster that decimates a department, there should always be officers capable of stepping up to the next rank. If your department is not training them to do so, it needs to be addressed and fixed. This is a segment of policing where corruption can become a serious issue. Politics should have no place in policing, but the reality is when it comes to these positions, there is likely to be some. I do not totally oppose and can understand the need for some political influence involved in the selection of an administrator. A civilian authority, such as a mayor, who oversees a municipality needs to have leaders whom they can trust and who are a part of their vision for the community. The leader of the police department is no exception. The problem arises when someone totally incompetent is placed in an administrative position. Even worse is when a corrupt leader is placed in charge so that a political, criminal enterprise can flourish.

So for those of you who came up through the ranks and are taking on the rank of an administrator, I encourage you NOT to drink the "forget where you came from" juice. Remember how you felt during your first days on the job. This is also the time to remember all the great ideas you had while you were working the streets, which you thought could have been done differently. You now have the opportunity not to just think of better ways to do something but to actually implement those changes.

To those from academia who did not come up through the ranks and feel you are deserving of this administrative job, please reconsider. If you are one of the few exceptions who actually can do the job, good luck. If, because of your pride or finances, you decide to go forward with this administrative job, humble yourself. Find out who the qualified officers are, those that maybe should have had the job you now have, and then surround yourself with them. Hold a meeting with your command staff and immediately get the white elephant out of the room. Be a man or woman, tell your staff what you think of them based on their folders, and then make it clear that you are now the top dog and that you plan on moving the department forward. Most police supervisors who were passed over for this job will probably have a brief period of reluctance but will soon go back to their roots of being good police officers and move on under your direction. Now is the time to acknowledge your shortcomings and seek their counsel. It is a biblical principle to seek council from many people, and this is one of those times you need it. If you choose not to follow the advice above and, as a means of realizing your grand scheme, decide to make those supervisors public enemy number one, be careful. You may just start a war that you are very unlikely to win in the long run. You will definitely not be building a cohesive police department if you go off on a personal vendetta.

Don't be the type of leader who is looking to write a thesis on a certain philosophy of policing and use your rank as a dictator to accomplish this. Don't be the type of leader who already has written a thesis and now wants to put it into effect regardless of the impact. If you have some great ideas, fine. Slowly implement them, and don't be too proud to adapt them to the needs of your agency, even if it causes you to veer off your original plan. Change is a good thing when done for the right reasons in the right way.

I was a big advocate of change. Increased efficiency and cost-effectiveness should always be the driving force. I will confess I was one who sometimes liked change for the sake of change. It served two purposes. It broke the "we've always done it this way" mind-set. It also created the mind-set for officers to think outside of the box. Additionally, it allowed for unification among the ranks to focus on a common goal. "Houle is a _____." Feel free to fill in the blank as I am sure I was called that word at one point or another. It allowed people to focus on a common problem—me. It was done not to create hardships but to create creative thinking. It would also provide for a distraction when morale would ebb.

As an administrator, you are going to set the tone of how your department operates internally. Under the discipline heading, you are going to establish just what is and what is not tolerated. I encourage you to foster an environment where officers can express themselves. As officers use discretion when applying the law to the general citizenry, do the same for your officers. When making decisions about this, you need to factor in the time and place it's being done, along with the motive. If things are done in good humor, it is a great way for officers to blow off steam. Police officers are very good at problem-solving, and this skill is used when applying it to internal stressors. I mentioned the war above. Cops can be pretty creative. For the most part of my career, we were fortunate to have an environment where practical jokes were accepted. As an opponent of community policing, I obviously ruffled some people's feathers. It didn't help when I would call them, never in public, the teddy bear squad because they had a nice stash of stuffed animals to hand out to children. Now obviously, I thought that was a good thing to do and handed out many myself, but it was a fun to banter back and forth. We were all on the same team, so internal joking should always keep that fact in mind—internal, not out in the public. Now one day, I entered my locked office in detectives, only to find the stuffed animal equivalent of Star Trek's "Tribbles" within. I mentioned having fun at work; this was one of those times. Now obviously, there was a rule and regulation about tampering with a supervisor's locked door, but if you are going to dish it out, you need to be able to take it. Aside from a good laugh and some photos (shown below), no further action was taken, nor should it have been. This is the part of setting the tone for what is and what is not acceptable. I even commended those officers whom I believed were the responsible parties for a job well done. It also reaffirmed the theory that criminals will often return to the scene of the crime as there were some uncommonly seen officers hanging around the detective division that morning when I opened my door.

Stuffed animal invasion, June 1998

Now if you are an administrator who, after reading this and seeing the above picture, is now saying, "I would never let that happen under my watch," I think you are going to have some problems administrating.

General orders, rules, regulations, policies, etc.—your department needs to have these clearly defined in a format that is available and understandable to all personnel within your department. This is not only a legal protection for your officers and the municipality; it is a written plan to achieve the goals of your agency. Guidelines need to be in place, but don't micromanage by trying to cover every aspect of the job. If the rules are too complex, they will lose their effectiveness, and confusion and apathy within the ranks may become a factor. Remember, with a great position comes great responsibility. Don't shun that responsibility as the buck now stops with you.

# ADMINISTRATION

# LOGISTICAL SUPPORT

Administrators are responsible for the structure of their police departments. They need to provide support for the officers under their charge and provide accountability to the elected officials and citizens of the community they work for. The structure and organization of a law enforcement agency is something that is assumed, but is it clearly defined and well documented? As an administrator, it is your job to make sure that logistics are available and implemented.

As with all the chapters of this book, I will not go into great details on this topic but touch on the basics. The first thing you need is a chain of command. Organizational charts are a great means of outlining this so that all involved can easily understand it. Once the chain of command is established, use it. Leadership starts at the top and by example. If you expect the officers in the ranks below you to respect the chain of command, you need to follow those principles too. The chain of command has information flowing both ways. Short of an on-scene emergency situation, directives should be passed on to the rank immediately below you and so on. The same is true going upward from the patrol officer to the sergeant, and onward and upward. This seems like such a simple process—why mention it? Most departments have an established chain of command, but unfortunately, this is not always the actual practice. Open-door policies for ranking officers should be limited to personal situations that don't need to be known by all. Open-door policies should not be used for the receipt or dissemination of police information. When you cut out the middle management, it not only violates the chain of command policy but also results in communication errors, which interfere with efficiency. If you as a ranking officer have an assignment for a patrol officer, the supervisors need to be made aware of it. If it's a confidential assignment, the supervisors don't need to know the particulars, but they need to know that an officer is not going to be available to handle calls. As my rank increased, my "gauntlet," as it was referred to by my coworkers, increased.

I encourage the practice of using a strong chain of command, but don't become an isolationist or an elitist. You are still a police officer. If you are driving by and see an officer stopping a car, stop. Be the officer's backup. Don't be afraid to interact with your officers, and use the principle of "two ears, one mouth" to get a feel for what is going on in your department, especially morale. Now after the car stop is finished and the officer starts telling you about a great idea they have, politely listen and then explain to them that they need to relay that information on to the sergeant. All careers have a group of people who like to butter up to the boss. Law enforcement is no exception. A strong chain of command is going to discourage this and allow them to become recognized based on the actual work they do not how likeable they are. By focusing them back to the chain of command, you will make them better police officers and maintain the chain of command that has been established.

A department's structure will include rules and regulations. You as the administrator are responsible for ensuring that these exist; that they are organized, comprehendible, and realistic. The language is important as you can be sure that any lawsuit brought against your department or your officers is going to be looking at that language with a fine toothcomb. One example that was brought to our attention dealt with our deadly force policy. An excerpt was "All other means are to be used before the use of deadly force."

Now that sounds good. I forgot the gentlemen's name, but we once had a consultant come in to review some of our policies. Upon reviewing this policy, he pointed out the fact that "all other means" included a lot of police tools that we did not have available to us at the time, stun guns being one. They were in existence, but our department had not purchased nor issued them. "ALL" every technology available was not necessarily available to us, so it should not have been in our policy. The language was changed: "All other means **available** are to be used before the use of deadly force."

*Available*—a simple word but the lack thereof could have resulted in an expensive legal liability for our department.

Your department's policies are going to be unique to your agency, but it is imperative that the basics be covered. The basics include those areas that involve your officer's safety and those where individual's rights are impacted by the police. Arrest procedures, use of force, use of deadly force, and vehicle pursuits need to be documented, be implemented, and institute training.

I cannot emphasize enough that as an administrator, you need to focus on officer safety. It seems, as time goes by, it has become acceptable for officers to become cannon fodder just so long as the status quo in the community is not interrupted. During the 1980s, the Rhode Island courts actually went under the premise that there was no such thing as an assault on a police officer, unless an injury was involved. Ridiculous. Just because I was wearing a uniform did not exclude me or any other officer from having the same rights under the law that everyone else did. Fortunately, this ruling was overturned, thanks in part to our local police union. When I was in the academy, Capt. Dennis McCarthy and many others stressed the following fact: **"It is better to be judged by twelve than carried by six."**

Maybe that is not a politically correct statement, but it is a very factual statement. I am not encouraging the days of the Wild West where it was "shoot first and ask questions later," but if you feel that your life or the life of another is in imminent jeopardy, you need to act quickly. Sometimes that action requires the use of deadly force. When you as a uniformed police officer are attempting to make an arrest and the arrestee assaults you, you have to assume that they want to inflict injuries upon you, which will allow for their escape. I don't believe in that "fight or flight" moment; the suspect is using a scaled "use of force" criteria where, at some point, they are going to stop resisting on their own free will. To ensure the safety of your officers and the public, make sure your officers have been issued the proper equipment. At the top of this list are handguns, bulletproof vests, stun guns, pepper spray ("man in the can"), and proper restraints. Ensure that the ammunition your officers are issued is suitable for the task at hand, which is stopping people quickly without causing unnecessary injury to others. You don't want bullets going through the suspect and hitting innocent civilians. There are some great studies on ammunition that you should review before making a purchase and a policy change. The one with the cool-looking ads might not actually perform as intended as I learned one time. I made a wrong decision, acknowledged it, and then changed it. The lives of your officers and your citizens are much more important than having to admit that you made a mistake. Make sure that officers have **readily available** good communication equipment, safe and reliable vehicles, long guns, riot gear, and other equipment they may need to save lives, starting with their own. *Readily available* does not mean locked up in a police station locker thirty minutes away from the scene where the items are needed. In addition to equipment, make sure the officers are working is a safe physical environment. Can they safely bring prisoners into a cell area? Are the working conditions inside of your police station safe, or is it a health hazard? After their basic safety is provided for, then you can focus on the other items you will need to run an efficient police department.

Planning and training need to be a part of your administration. If you have the personnel to establish a planning and training unit, great. If you don't have that luxury, you need to assign someone to this task, even if it is yourself. Just because a policy is instituted or when a situation happens involving that particular policy does not mean that it never needs to be reviewed again. You want to be ahead of the curve, not doing damage control. All rules, regulations, and policies should be reviewed on a regular basis. Court decisions will have great impact on what is and what is not allowed by police officers. At a minimum, all rules, regulations, and policies should be reviewed annually. If they are obsolete, then they need to be updated or deleted. A perfect example of this lack of review can be found in many state laws. These outdated and duplicative laws may be humorous to look at, like a "dueling" statute still on the books in the twenty-first century, but they weaken and confuse the law. We actually charged some people under this dueling statute in the 1990s. It was definitely an attention-getter, but it was a means of dissuading people to show up for scheduled fights after school, even though it was an antiquated law—problem-solving policing, with a little humor thrown in. I am amazed that the "rule of law" that involves the principle that all citizens are supposed to know the law has not been more aggressively challenged by a good defense attorney. Don't let your rules and regulations get outdated.

Planning and training obviously includes training, but how often is training actually done? Training your officers is an essential duty of administrators. Training should encompass every aspect of police work that an officer will have to deal with on a regular basis. Training can be as simple as spending five minutes on a topic in roll call to sending officers to schools to become certified in a specialized field. Officer-training programs are essential. When I got on the job, I had four days with a training officer, and then I was on my own. I was fortunate to have Cpl. Stephen Crowley as my field training officer (FTO)—trial by fire. I think it made us good police officers, but in this day and age, the officer training program needs to be comprehensive. Regardless of whether training is done in-house or by an outside entity, all training needs to be documented. This training documentation needs to be stored in a manner that is beneficial to the officers, the administration, and the citizens. In other words, training certificates should not only consist of a shoe box of certificates sitting on the floor of an officer's locker.

Administrators need to focus on efficiency and cost-effectiveness for your agency, with the well-being of your officers being paramount. Having worked on the ground level, hopefully, you are well aware of the policies and procedures that are not as efficient as they could be. A good way to implement change is not to simply state a problem but to provide alternative solutions at the same time as well. Note to administrators: this is a time you need to be humble and to listen to those under you command. Most great innovations in law enforcement came from the people who performed the task and were innovative enough to present a good alternative. Guess what? If your officers do a good job, people will look upon you as a good leader. Inspire creativity within your department. Yes, there will need to be a balance, and you also need to be able to say no. When you say no, state your logic behind your decision and thank the officer for their input.

One area I found wasteful as a patrolman was the number of forms with the same information for each arrest. This was in the days of typewriters. We had to fill out a physical description sheet, an arrest card, an arrest jacket, and an evidence card and book the arrestee. Most of all these forms required the same information. One of my first actions as a sergeant was a proposal to have one duplicate form with all this data, utilizing a carbon paper. (For you younger people, carbon paper was the equivalent of multiple copies.) I got a quote from the local printing company we utilized and had a sample prepared. This was presented and discussed at a staff meeting, and shortly thereafter, Chief Winquist implemented it. The amount of time we saved, being out of service typing information, was greatly reduced, and we were able to increase the amount of time officers could spend on the street. Don't just point out an area that can be improved; provide a viable solution.

Throughout my command career, I would frequently get similar suggestions. Lt. James Trail once proposed using a waterproof digital camera to use at arson scenes. Again, he presented me with the facts and prices. Not only did we purchase this and started using it, but also through this effort, Lieutenant Trail brought the entire detective division into the age of digital photography, much sooner than most departments in the region. Encourage creative thought and allow your officers the ability to present new ideas. If their presentation is not inspiring, help them better prepare their idea. This is the job of a supervisor—to teach officers under your command how not only to do their job but also to make a good presentation. You need to allow officers under your command to grow. As I mentioned earlier, there should always be somebody qualified to assume your position. If you have spent the time on teaching others and they have successfully learned, be happy. Consider your actions as a success. Even if those you teach go on to be your supervisor, relish in the fact that you were a part of their growth.

# ADMINISTRATION

# CRIME MAPPING TARGETS CRIMES

Administrators are responsible for the department's record-keeping system. You need to have a functional system that records all crimes and incidents that your officers are dealing with. It is up to the administration to install, maintain, and ensure compliance with whatever system is put in place. It is the administration that needs to regularly review this system and determine if changes need to be made to make it efficient for the officers and the citizens who depend upon it. When a citizen needs a police report, it should be readily available. The response should not be "Officer so and so took that report. It's on his desk somewhere, but he's off today. Come back tomorrow."

Your records system needs to have a purpose, and one of those purposes is for public access to reports. There needs to be guidelines established on what reports and what victim information in reports are released. It should go without saying, but reports related to active, ongoing investigations are not part of the public record. People need police reports primarily for insurance purposes when they have been involved in an accident or are the victim of a crime. As part of instilling good will with the public, they should be able to get reports in a timely manner. Most people work during the day, so citizens who have already experienced hardship should not have to take time out of work to get a report. They should also be able to get a copy of a police report without taking out a loan. It's disgusting what some police departments charge victims for a copy of a report when they are already a victim. A small administrative fee is fine, but providing copies of police reports should not be a moneymaker for the municipality.

Although not all, many crimes will have a pattern. The only way to identify these patterns is to make sure you are gathering the correct information related to the crime. This includes the date, day of the week, time, weather, and location. For crimes against a person, you need gather information on the victim. Most victim information gathered will be basic: address, place of employment, sex, age, race, etc. What you as the investigating officer need to be aware of are other factors. Although these factors should not be a part of a police database, they could be very well be factors in a crime pattern. Sadly, people are still targeted by criminals based on their race, faith, beliefs, and sexual orientation.

The more data you have to compare crimes, the better your success in targeting crime. Your technology should be such that based on queries, it can formulate an algorithm to predict crime. If your database cannot do this, then you need to have a system, even if it is someone reviewing paper reports, to identify crime patterns and formulate theories about the crime pattern.

Back in 1979, Capt. Richard Ferreria and Ptl. Archie Andrade have a system in place where three-by-five index cards were used in the supplication of the new computer system database that was in its trial stage. Police officers are, by nature, reluctant to change. At the time, everyone was moaning about gathering all this "useless data" from victims; however, it was still gathered. As the system developed, we all could see the value in this information, and the department as a whole was able to target specific areas. The department also learned to have faith in the database, and the three-by-five cards went by the wayside.

Electronic information is wonderful, but there needs to be a means of disseminating this information to all officers, especially those working on the street. A technician forwarding a six-page report about a crime pattern to administrators is great, but is it reaching the officers on the street in a timely, comprehendible, and concise manner? This information needs to be condensed to the basics so that officers can act without getting bogged down in reading a long technical analysis. What, when, and where did these crimes occur? Your officers are problem solvers, so when they have the information, they can now act on it. Supervisors can now relocate staff to address these problems. Officers are overwhelmed with information every day. The simpler this information can be communicated to them, the better.

We would use crime maps for our major crimes. I'm sure today it can be done electronically, but we did not have that luxury at the time. (I further assume they do now as one of my retirement gifts from Lt. Tom Rush was the box of nicely sorted pins we used for this purpose.) For our major crimes, we would take the data on target crimes and maintained a pin map—a paper map of the entire city, which was updated daily—on the wall. Specific color pins, each color representing a specific type of crime, were used for specific crimes. One quick look in seconds at this map was enough to let officers know where to focus their efforts. When the pins turned into clusters of pins, officers could now really narrow their focus. It was a visual reminder, plainly in the view of officers daily.

If your department does not have some system to identify target crimes, you need to implement one. It can be a basic paper map or paper report, or it can be an app your officers can easily access online. Regardless of the method you implement, it needs to be updated constantly. You want your officers to solve and prevent crime, so you as the administrator need to make this information readily available to them in a format that is accessible and understandable.

CHAPTER

25

# TECHNOLOGY IN LAW ENFORCEMENT

The advances of technology has had an enormous impact on law enforcement over the past century. Even in my twenty-four-year career, the changes were amazing—facial recognition programs, AFIS fingerprint systems, DNA analysis, digital photography, etc. Technology is great, and with it comes responsibility. We need to be responsible to the citizens we protect to uphold the Fourth Amendment. Yes, I know, for those who worked with me, my favorite line was "the Constitution was a ship floating in Boston Harbor." Some law students would tell me the Constitution was a breathing living thing. I say if it is living and breathing or has elastic properties, stretch and twist that elastic as much as possible. Regardless of your view, it truly is something we need to respect. Although I like it stretched as far as possible to benefit law enforcement, it still exists, and some of the current technology needs to be used with caution.

Another area your police department needs to be responsible with regarding technology is not to buy everything a vendor sells. If you want to find a victim of a great scam, you might not have to look any further than your own police department. I saw it over and over during my career. First is the technology in its beta stage. Some slick salesman will come calling, offering your department to be on the frontline of the newest technology, complete with an introductory price.

Like any technology, let someone with a bigger ego try it out first, and let them work out the bugs. Your department can then assess it, determine the cost, and decide if it will, in fact, cut costs and increase efficiency. One example I saw was when our department switched over to computer-automated dispatching and computer-generated reporting. This was going to be the end of paperwork and the streamlining of the whole process. We were sold a bill of goods from a company that had all the frills and spills in place—cool logos, nice suits, brand-new SUVs, and a slick-talking salesman. The trouble was the system did not work. Every time the sales rep came in, the demonstration was always done on his own laptop. At one point, he was publicly challenged to do his "tricks" with our own hardware. He refused to use the in-house system—our desktops uploaded with his company's software that we were supposed to be using for the day-to-day operations. The fact that he would not use our equipment spoke volumes. My department spent tens of thousands of dollars on a program that did not work. It was so bad that fraud charges were successfully brought against the company.

After years of this debacle, wasted time and money, we selected the company IMC. This company had no frills but a system in place. Changes were not made easily. Although frustrating, it was proven over time that a system needed to have constants to be interactive and consistent. You could actually retrieve data to provide useful data for the entire department. Eventually, much of the region switched over to this system, which remained consistent throughout this transition. This not only allowed for a user-friendly in-house system but also provided for the easy interchange of data among other departments with whom we would work with.

You should also encourage your officers to be up to date on the latest technology. I personally have to give credit to officers Cpl. Steve Crowley, Capt. Joseph Broadmeadow, Cpl. Cathy Tabella-Sailor, Lt. Steve Enos, and Lt. James Trail. They all had a great influence on pushing our department into the computer age while I was there. Many of us, including me, were very suspect of the new changes they proposed, but their efforts put us on the cutting edge of technology in law enforcement in Rhode Island at the time.

Although I eventually became a big proponent of technology, I urge you not to get rid of the paper reports. Almost everything you enter in a computer system should be printed out and stored somewhere. If you are not going to print everything, at least those records relating to major crimes and criminals should have a hard copy somewhere. This includes digital photographs. All computer systems are vulnerable to internal malfunction or external hacking. Because your computer system is frozen should not mean your operation is frozen, particularly during a major investigation when timely data is essential to save a life. All systems are vulnerable at some point. There are some, albeit a few, criminals who will have the financial means to secure a hacker to remove the records relating to their arrest from your system, and the obvious is no evidence, no conviction.

Technology is not going away anytime soon. As all soldiers know how to fire a rifle, all police officers should have a working knowledge of the technology available to them and to the criminal element and how to handle this technology. It could be as basic as not touching a computer until an expert gets there. The more sophisticated the criminal who is using the technology is, the more sophisticated the fail safes on his system will be. This is one area, depending on the size of your department, where you might want to have a specialized unit. Whether you have a special unit or not, you need to have policies in place that encompass technology used in the commission of a crime. This is also a point where you can get out in the community, find the true geeks, and seek their assistance when warranted. Obviously, you need to follow the proper protocol, warrants, etc., but some of these geeks would probably love the challenge of getting into and extracting data from a suspect's computer. If you are on the job or planning on applying for the job, focus all those college electives toward the area of information technology. If you are a natural geek, hone those skills with degrees and certificates that will allow you to be an expert in a court of law and provide one more asset to your police department.

Technology is going to continue to expand at an exponential rate, and you need to make sure that you and your department are ready to use this technology to serve the public good.

# CHAPTER 26

# POLICE FUNERALS

# THE FINAL GOODBYE

Police funerals are one of those things that people on the outside just don't quite understand. They are steeped in tradition and not easily explained. It is something between an old-fashioned Irish wake and a Viking funeral rite. It is one of the most formal, saddest moments you can imagine. Lt. Steve Crowshaw once said that police funerals are designed to bring the emotionally toughest to a point of tears. He said cops don't cry often, yet if the shear masses of brothers and sisters gathered or the bagpipes playing don't get you crying, then the playing of taps or the gun salute will. He was right.

Police funerals are a way of honoring those who have died while serving in one of the most dangerous and important professions in the world. It is not always a line of duty death either. Any officer who wears or wore a shield should be honored with a police funeral when they pass.

Shortly after getting on the job, I quickly learned the importance of attending a fellow officer's funeral. Maj. Wayne Gallagher, Capt. Bill Sloyer, Lt. Steve Crowshaw, and Sgt. Gordon Remond were all very instrumental in making you volunteer for these. I loosely use the word *volunteer*. At first, that sixth sense told me that if I didn't go, the next shift was not going to be ideal. At the same time, I will point out how glad I was that these officers fostered this trait in me and my coworkers at an early time in my career.

A collage of the memorial outside of the East Providence Police
Department, honoring all those officers who have passed on

At first, what I found peculiar was that most of these funerals were
for officers from other towns, cities, and states. It was not until after I
attended a few of these that I realized the importance of this gesture.
It was really not until I personally experienced it to know how uplifting
this is to a grieving family. Let's be honest. You just finished a midnight
shift; the last thing you feel like doing is to spend the day driving for an
hour to stand in the sun, with a woolen jacket on for hours in formation,
and then marching distances measured by miles in-step (attempting to
anyway) to honor a fallen officer. This is where you have to let integrity
and camaraderie rule over your feelings. This trait was ingrained in me so
much that to this day, I feel negligent if I can't stuff myself into my dress
uniform and attend the services for one of my own comrades. I actually
tear up while writing this, thinking of all the memories of the ones I have
attended. If you are a citizen and happen to witness one of these events and
notice all the officers who are hanging around before the formal ceremony,

laughing and joking, maybe throwing down a beer, don't judge. That is our way of dealing with grief because we all know that it is by the grace of God that we are not the one in the coffin. Stick around for the formal ceremony and then see how many are laughing and joking.

Our department had a great reputation for honoring our fallen brother and sister officers throughout New England. This was evident one time when Chief Norman Miranda once went to an event in Boston, Massachusetts. While attempting to find parking in an area where parking is prime, he was talking to a Boston police officer. The officer's comment to him was "East Providence, the professional mourners. Yeah, follow me. I have a place for you to park (with a big smile on his face)." That was police lingo for saying, "Thank you, brother. I really appreciate what your department does."

If you are an administrator, an officer's death is really the time you are going to need to be a leader. If it is one of your own who has died, your officers are suffering, and you need to serve them. If it is a line of duty death, your first task is to find the person responsible. Don't be afraid to seek assistance from outside agencies in this task. Most often they will be more than willing to send whatever assistance you need. On the same note, when this happens in another agency, be the first to offer assistance, and ignore your budget for a period. Emotions run high when an officer is killed, and you as the leader need to manage this.

Your next task, done simultaneously, is to reach out to the officer's family. For the time being, they are your new family, and treat them as such. Unfortunately, I experienced this when my daughter Kimberly, a sworn correctional officer at the Adult Correctional Institute (ACI), was killed in a motor vehicle accident. My family was adopted not only by the Rhode Island Department of Corrections but also by the East Providence Police Department. CO John Bray of the ACI and Lt. Raymond Blinn of EPPD, along with hundreds of other officers, were by our family's side for days. I will never forget the day of the funeral. Most families have limos. We had Chief Paquette, Major Dubois, Captain Hogan, Captain Charbonneau, Captain Frazier, Lieutenant Hall, Sergeant Andrews, and Sergeant Atwell. Not only was it comforting for my entire family, but also it was a statement to those around us of the bond that exists in law enforcement.

As an administrator, you also need to start making logistical plans about how your officer's wake and funeral are going to be handled. The family's wishes need to be paramount. You can address some logistical concerns you may have with them, but in the end, their wishes need to be honored. Based on their requests, you can then make your plans. Don't assume that everything will just work out. Have a plan. You need to gather your command staff and your police union representatives and start delegating. Everyone should be given an assignment, and you need to meet with them regularly to provide updates so all are on the same page; incident command. If you have never experienced a department funeral, there are a lot of factors that need to be considered. You can expect a large turnout of officers from other departments. If the officer was killed in the line of duty, you can expect an even larger turnout of officers from around the country and maybe even other countries. In New England, representatives from the Royal Canadian Mounted Police were frequently in attendance at law enforcement funerals. You need to have a plan on what to do with this influx of people.

You need to have your officers set up an honor guard, even if you don't have a formal honor guard, to be with the officer's body while on display and until the final stage. This means multiple officers need to be assigned to this. Your officers are hopefully going to want to attend all the services, and you need to make arrangements to allow them to do this. This is the time you seek out assistance from your neighboring municipalities, along with the state police force, to cover the day-to-day operations of the police department so your officers can pay their respects and have some time to process their feelings.

You need to plan for those officers who will be coming to the services. Again, if it was a line of duty death, depending upon your geographic area, these visiting officers could easily number in the thousands. Information about where to go, park, and stage needs to be disseminated ahead of time. You should also make sure arrangements are made to provide them with basic necessities—toilets, water, etc.—at the location they muster. Lodging may be an issue for some, so this information should also be disseminated in advance. Reach out to your local hotels as I am sure they would be willing to assist you in this task. Plan the routes that the officers will be using during the wake and the funeral. Whether they march on foot or are in a vehicle procession or a combination of both, you are likely going to need to have someone coordinate with public works to shut down roads and make the proper notifications to the local media. In the end, make sure you are a good host and thank these officers for coming. Provide for a reception to be held at the end of the services. This is the time that officers can truly vent their feelings and provide encouragement to your officers.

My daughter's death was another time when it was hard for me to try and explain this bond that exists within the law enforcement community. While there was a wave of officers in and out of our home, there were also many civilian friends and family by our side. One of these was my cousin Dick who had spent his life in the business world. After the funeral, he came up to me and asked, very perplexed, "I thought you had retired." To which I replied, "I did, four years ago." He then asked, "Then what can you do for these officers?" To which I replied, "Absolutely nothing at all. It's a family matter. It's what I did with them over the years."

If you are a civilian and an officer has been killed and the department is mourning, this is NOT the time to have trivial complaints about your police department. Don't ask why they are shutting down the city or why it is taking a little longer for an officer to show up or why an officer from another city showed up. If you tend to have an attitude toward law enforcement and just can't help making a wise crack to an officer, I encourage you, this is the time to bite your tongue and not make that remark. By doing so, it will benefit all involved.

In remembrance of the East Providence Police officers killed in the line of duty:

Maj. Alister McGregor, 1958–2001
Ptl. James R. Caruso, 1924–1958
Ptl. Peter F. Pepin, 1882–1922

Not in the line of duty, but his tragic accident affected us all deeply:

Sgt. Gordon "Ray" Remond, 1947–1990

The following page has a collage of pictures of our brother and sister officers who attended the funeral of Rhode Island correctional officer Kimberly Ann Houle, badge 1639, January 27, 2006. The photos are courtesy of CO Alfredo Maldonado Jr. who dedicated his time to taking these and many more. Other photos given to us by Correctional Officer Maldonado can be found at www.kimhoule.tripod.com.

# POLICE UNIONS AND
# FRATERNAL ORGANIZATIONS

M any people will complain about the power of police unions and, to a lesser extent, fraternal organizations. I was and still am a proud member of Rhode Island Fraternal Order of Police (FOP), lodge no. 1, and I was also privileged to be a member of the International Brotherhood of Police Officers.

I was not known as a union activist, especially after I made rank, but I would never have made rank without God's intervention and a strong union in place. Aside from providing for a quality work environment and a halfway decent pay, the most important part of a union in a law enforcement agency is to keep a lid on corruption. Without unions allowing officers to act objectively and independently, corruption can easily flourish. Even with our union, the frequency of political interference into criminal investigations was noticeable. Whenever someone who was politically connected was arrested or issued a violation, you better be sure to dot all your *I*s and cross all your *T*s.

The Rhode Island judicial system had great integrity and objectivity the vast majority of the time, but it was sad to see how it would occasionally cater to certain individuals. Capt. Richard Frazier and I once had a drunk-driving case dismissed because neither of us testified that the telephone "worked." We both testified at length that the suspect was given the opportunity to make a telephone call and, in fact, had made a telephone call, but we never testified that the telephone in the police station actually worked. Aside from this, the case was very solid, and the judge had to really stretch to find this loophole to dismiss the case.

They had originally attempted to fix the case by not having either of us subpoenaed to court. Because the suspect was so adamant about the fact he knew the right people to get it "fixed," I made it a point to call the court to find out when the court date was. When that date came, we just happened to show up. It was funny to look at the reactions of the defendant, the defense lawyer, and the prosecutor when they saw us standing there, ready to testify. I will never forget the judge yelling from behind closed doors, "I'm not touching this with a ten-foot pole!"

On another occasion, I had issued a speeding violation to a neighboring mayor. Never mind his license showed that he lived in a city other than the one he was mayor of, and never mind he never showed up in court for his hearing; the judge stopped the hearing on her own, midway through my testimony. She had the audacity to ask if it was, in fact, the mayor of such and such a city. What I wanted to say to her was "Of course, he's the crooked mayor we are always hearing about in the news. Why do you think I gave him a ticket?"

However, I just shrugged, pointed out the city listed on the license as being different from the one she mentioned, and continued to testify. In the end, she had no choice but to find him guilty (responsible) in absentia for the violation, even though you could tell she was very uncomfortable about doing so. On a happier note, for totally unrelated matters, he was later indicted by a federal grand jury on corruption charges, and she was removed from the bench for judicial misconduct.

The point of these two stories is not to point out deficiencies in the judicial system but to point out that without a good union in place, Captain Frazier and I would more than likely have been subject to arbitrary disciplinary action or maybe even terminated. Giving a ticket to a mayor might result in a transfer to the midnight shift. Police unions provide for a stable work environment that discourages political interference with the daily operations, both internally and externally. Schedules, assignments, promotions, etc., are based on guidelines negotiated by unions to prevent and discourage preferential treatment and unwarranted punitive punishment.

Did you ever ask yourself what your police officers are making? As far as dangerous jobs go, we are probably making a little more than our men and women serving in the military in combat across the globe. Our military personnel are not making much at all, compared with the sacrifices they have to endure. I am tired of hearing about how some professional athletes making millions of dollars are now suffering because they were not warned ahead of time about traumatic brain injury. I don't think one needs a medical degree to assume that if you keep banging your head over and over, something bad is going to happen to your brain. What warnings do we give to our military personnel and first responders before they sign up? Do you think they say, "Listen, if you take this job, you may lose your life or some of your limbs, and you are more than likely to suffer long-term physical and emotional injuries that you will carry with you for the rest of your life. Do you still want the job? Oh, by the way, if you take the job, you are not going to make close to what the professional athlete is earning, even the one who is keeping the bench warm"?

Although police officers are not going to normally make the big bucks, police unions strive to make sure officers are compensated appropriately. The bottom line for most police officers is to slug it out at an average pay, get beat up physically and emotionally for twenty years, and then look forward to a decent retirement. Based on their sacrifice, I don't think this is an unreasonable expectation. I get so tired of listening to some people whining about the benefits police officers receive. Often these whiners are the same ones who have spent their life going from one company to another, cutting the bottom line, and lining their pockets, often at the expense of line employees. These "corporate raiders" tend not to show any loyalty nor compassion to the people their actions have an impact on. We were fortunate to have Lt. Ralph Ezovski as our union advocate for many years. I believe Ralph was and is such an advocate for working people after he saw how his parents were treated during their working years by some of these "corporate raiders." He took the injustices he saw in the past and, instead of getting angry, did something positive. Prior to Ralph, we were fortunate to have Ptl. Anthony Patalano who was instrumental in bringing the FOP to Rhode Island and setting up FOP lodge no. 1. He was then followed by two great advocates—Cpl. Francis Hurley and Lt. Steven Crowshaw. We are all very thankful for the sacrifices these officers made.

Police organizations are very much needed in this society. We need to know that our officers are given the same judicial review that is given to criminals. They are also important in bringing national trends to light, which benefit all citizens. It is through much hard work that these organizations have made the profession first a profession and, most importantly, provided for a safer work environment. Unions and fraternal organizations also foster that camaraderie within our profession, which builds that thin blue line that I will discuss later.

Police unions are also very instrumental in protecting the rights of the officers who are making life-or-death decisions in split seconds daily. During these split seconds, these officers are required to protect and respect the rights of those they are interacting with. The person whom the police chased for ten miles at high speeds and who then, when finally stopped, decides to assault the police to enable his escape is presumed innocent until proven guilty. So in spite of what the officers observed and experienced, if this person's rights are violated during this process, he will go free. This same criteria should apply to police officers when they are accused of a wrongdoing. That is where unions are an integral part of your law enforcement agency. If officers are concerned they are going to lose their jobs for doing their job, they are going to be less likely to be proactive and take the appropriate risks.

In the early and midpart of the twentieth century, maybe it is still happening somewhere, if an officer were to arrest a politically connected individual, they may be out of a job or be reassigned or be demoted. Violations of department rules and regulations were also handled randomly, without the assistance of union representation. Although before my time, there were some senior officers who worked with me who would share their stories of what happened when a union was not in place. When a departmental violation occurred, they would be punished by receiving "hours." Basically, if shifts needed to be filled, officers were ordered to work their "hours" to cover that shift. It was a very indiscriminate and unscrupulous way of punishment.

One complaint often heard from the uninformed when a department is out of control is that the police union is too strong and the police chief is not allowed to administer discipline within the ranks. Nothing could be further from the truth. If an officer violates criminal laws or departmental regulations, an investigation should be done. This investigation should be designed to seek out the truth. If, in fact, after a thorough investigation, there is enough evidence against an officer to warrant such, then criminal or departmental charges should be filed against that officer. To say there is no place for police unions is to say there is no place for defense attorneys. It is how the American justice system is designed, and police officers should not be exempt from this system. Oftentimes when an administrator is complaining, they cannot do anything because "the union has my hands tied"; it is, in fact, because they were not very good investigators while in the ranks or, worse, were never investigators. Furthermore, they may have surrounded themselves with incompetent staff. On a side note, administrators, don't surround yourself and always listen to the advice of people whom you like and who are like-minded to you. I enjoyed having a lot of people around me who didn't always agree with me and who were not afraid to say no or to tell me my idea was ridiculous. It was refreshing to hear their views, and it was nice to know they felt comfortable enough to honestly express them to me, regardless of their rank. The Bible teaches that it is godly to seek the counsel of many. Proverbs 11:14, 12:15, and 15:22 are just some I encourage you to review. That does not mean it should be a democracy. Once counsel is listened to, you still need to make a decision, as talked about earlier in this book. Because of the fact that I respected their input, they, in turn, respected my decisions. Even when a decision was made against their advice, they would follow through with it.

So back to the point, when internal matters arise, you as the administrator need to conduct a proper and timely investigation. If this is not done or cannot be done because of incompetence, blame yourself. When the problems persist within your agency and the cancer gets worse, don't blame the police union. Don't use the police union as a scapegoat when what is really needed is some self-introspection.

In Rhode Island, we are fortunate to have the "Law Enforcement Officers' Bill of Rights" created in 1976. It is found in the *Rhode Island General Laws*, chapter 42-28.6. It provides for very specific procedures to be followed, which not only protect the dignity of an accused officer but also provide the municipality guidelines to ensure discipline is done quickly and that punishment is appropriate to the violation. Many states have adopted similar laws, and if your state does not have one, I would encourage you to contact your elected officials to implement something similar.

Citizens of a municipality also benefit when there is a strong police union in place. With a decent salary and benefit package in place, you are going to attract more candidates. More candidates equate to the municipality's ability to select officers from a larger pool of qualified people. It also provides you comfort, knowing that officers are allowed to act in an objective manner and will strive to make you and your community safer.

# THE THIN BLUE LINE

# THE LAW ENFORCEMENT FAMILY

As described by Wikipedia (2017),

The Thin Blue Line is a symbol used by law enforcement, originating in the United Kingdom but now prevalent in the United States and Canada to commemorate fallen, and to show support for, the living law enforcement officers and to symbolize the relationship of law enforcement in the community as the protectors of fellow civilians from criminal elements. It is an analogy to the term *Thin Red Line*.

In the United Kingdom, the primary use of the badge is as a mark of respect for fallen police officers / staff. However, it also represents the thin line between order and chaos—this has become a large topic of interest in recent years, as severe cuts to government spending on public services has led to a dramatic decline in the number of police officers and staff in the UK. A variation of the emblem places a horizontal thin blue line across a Union Jack rendered in black and white. The sale of badges with this emblem is used to raise money for families of police officers that have died in the line of duty.

In the United States of America, each stripe on the emblem represents certain respective figures: the blue center line represents law enforcement, the top black stripe represents the public and the bottom represents the criminals. The idea behind the graphic is that law enforcement (the blue line) is what stands between the violence and victimization by criminals and the would-be victims of crime. (End of description)

Law enforcement officers, in fact, represent that barrier that prevents those who want to do whatever they want to whomever they want whenever they want the inability to do so. The line may be thin, but it is almost unbreakable and extends across most of the world. Ask any police officer who has traveled the globe what interactions took place between them and their counterparts once they both realized they were a part of that thin blue line.

Law enforcement is one huge family. As stated throughout this book, with the exception of maybe the military and fire services, I don't think you will find such a universal camaraderie existing among such a diverse group. I cannot thoroughly explain it, but like the sixth sense, it exists.

Our code for an officer needing assistance was "10-3." If you are a supervisor and you hear this, even if you are not a believer, this is the moment you want to start praying, not so much for the safety of the officer calling for help but the massive wave on the way to help them. If you saw the movie *When We Were Soldiers*, you might remember the scene when actor Mel Gibson called in on the radio, "Broken arrow." If you remember the shit storm that soon followed this, this is what is now going on in your city. Every officer who heard that dropped everything they were doing and was on their way to help a fellow officer. (If not, this is that time to reflect to see if you are in the right job. If you are an administrator and this type of activity is strongly discouraged, it's time to retire.) Those officers are now in a family-preservation mode, working mostly from instinct, with high levels of adrenaline pumping through their bodies.

If you are one of those officers in the ever-growing, ever-speeding wave ascending onto the scene, FOCUS. Yes, I know it won't be easy, but remember now is the time to channel that energy, gather your thoughts, and get there without killing yourself or someone else. It is also the time to vigilantly enter a situation but still use your brain above all else.

This could happen if you let your adrenaline control you.

Having been on the initiating end of this call for help more than once, what a relief to hear that first siren and watch the cavalry show up. It was sheer coincidence, but Lt. Dan Evans frequently seemed to be working when the going was getting tough for me. As soon as I saw him arrive, there was a little voice in my head that said, "It's going to be all right now," and it always was. He was a man of pure business yet composed and was able to quickly deescalate a scene.

I always wondered why there is such a vocal minority who don't like the police. I'm not talking here about most criminals. Most criminals have great respect for their police and appreciate the job they do. I can't tell you how many times somebody we arrested later became a victim, trusting the police to solve their problems. This is a reflection of the respect you earn while doing your job. There are many other groups of people who just don't like law enforcement. Usually, they are the found predominantly on the extreme left, but there are large segments on the extreme right as well. When police misconduct is in the news, the negative implication of the thin blue line is interjected. I am not sure what the rationale for this deep hatred is within these groups. Maybe they are spoiled brats who grew up, and now the police are getting in their way of doing what they want. Maybe it is all the social scientists who have been working unsuccessfully on social justice for years, and all of a sudden, this group forms, "law enforcement", that coexists and works for a common goal. Maybe it is just anarchists who realize that law enforcement is the agency that actually maintains the order in a society.

This thin blue line has proven to overcome many of the biases that exist in our world. We don't look at ourselves as male-female, gay-straight, black, white, red or yellow. Neither do we look at ourselves as Christian,

Jew, Muslim, Atheist, etc. We look at ourselves as cops first and foremost. There certainly was a period where not all groups were accepted into the law enforcement family, but brave people entered the ranks and EARNED that respect. During my career, I saw the increase in the number of female, Black, Asian, gay, and lesbian officers who became a part of the law enforcement family. I know it was not easy for those pioneers, but they had the courage to follow their heart. I realize there are still issues of inequality and bias within departments, but overall, we get along, treat one another as family, and work toward a common goal—not a lot of social science intervention, just hard work.

Now just like most families, the police family can have a lot of animosity within at times. Whenever a large group of people are together for long periods, someone is eventually going to get on someone else's nerves. I watched as one time, one of my coworkers was getting under another officer's skin to a point where the latter thrust kick the other across a driveway. The difference here is the next day, the two were working side by side, having a coffee at the beginning of the shift. There may have been officers you might not socialize with on a regular basis off-duty, but when moving day came, you were there to move. If their child was in need of a bone marrow transplant, you were there registering. Regardless of how officers interact on a personal level, there is always that family bond that exists. Just like a civilian family's rivalries disappear when an outsider steps in, so is it in the police family.

I could fill volumes of books with individual incidents to try and relay this bond that exists in the police community, but I won't. However, I hope you get the idea that the "thin blue line" is not only good for police officers but also good for the citizens of a community.

CHAPTER

29

# WHY COPS HATE YOU

S hortly after graduating from the police academy in 1979, one of my classmates forwarded me a short article with the title "Why Cops Hate You: If You Have to Ask, Get out of the Way." The original author Chuck Milland is a retired lieutenant from the Baltimore, Maryland, police department. This same article, with a few edits, can now also be found on the website, outlining the history of the Baltimore City Police Department (BPD). The website is not affiliated with BPD and is maintained by retired Det. Kenneth Driscoll. Driscoll is a highly decorated member of that department, who is now permanently disabled as the result of an on-the-job injury, yet his dedication to serve his brother and sister police officers continues. Ken has given me permission to publish the article as found on the site. I encourage you to visit the site at http://baltimorecitypolicedept.org/citypolice/bpd-history.

I wanted to share this article with you so you too could enjoy what I believe are some very humorous observations. A lot of the content is dated in the late seventies, but I believe it points out some things that civilians could do to make the lives of police officers as well as their own lives a little bit better.

When I taught at our civilian police academy, I would hand out the full article to the participants, with the colorful language redacted. Most all found it humorous, but there was always one in the group who would say something like "I don't think this is accurate."

I would simply say that it was meant for humor. What I wanted to say is the article is referring to people who may be just like you. Enjoy the humor, don't be self-absorbed, and don't overanalyze it—*intelligencia* at its best. I often find that some of the most educated people can be the dumbest when it comes to basic life skills. I strongly encourage you to further your education throughout your life, but please maintain some common sense. I once told a young man in college not to become so smart that he forgets how to pick his nose. The response indicated that he was already lost. I had to hear for fifteen minutes how nose picking is not only impractical but also not hygienic. Yes, no kidding, but it works. Remove the bat in the cave, breathe better, and then wash your hands. This is the same person who will consume raw fish loaded with worms and rationalize how cool it is. As you go out to invent the molecular transporter, don't ignore some of the earlier inventions, such as controlled fire, also known as cooking, and learn how to take things in context.

The article below is not politically correct, but it reflects the contemporary culture of the 1970s. Even if you are not familiar with the culture of the seventies—portable TVs, *Dirty Harry*, tape players, public telephones, etc.—I believe you will still get the gist of what the article intends to convey to the average citizen.

## WHY COPS HATE YOU
### If You Have to Ask, Get out of the Way
### CHUCK MILAND

Have you ever been stopped by a traffic cop, and while he was writing a ticket or giving you a warning, you got the feeling that he would just love to yank you out of the car, right through the window, and smash your face into the front fender?

Have you ever had a noisy little spat with someone, and a cop cruising by calls, "Everything all right over there?"

Did you maybe sense that he really hoped everything was not all right, that he wanted one of you to answer, "No officer, this idiot's bothering me"? That all he was looking for was an excuse to launch himself from the cruiser and play a drum solo on his skull with his nightstick?

Did you ever call the cops to report a crime—maybe someone stole something from your car or broke into your home—and the cops act as if it were your fault? That they were sorry the crook didn't rip you off for more? That instead of looking for the culprit, they'd rather give you a shot in the chops for bothering them in the first place?

If you've picked up on this attitude from your local sworn protectors, it's not just paranoia. They actually don't like you. In fact, the cops don't just dislike you, they hate your guts! Incidentally, for a number of very good reasons.

First of all, civilians are so damn stupid. They leave things lying around, just begging thieves to steal them. They park cars in high crime areas and leave portable TVs, cameras, wallets, purses, coats, luggage, grocery bags and briefcases in plain view on the seat. Oh sure, maybe they'll remember to close all the windows and lock all the doors, but do you know how easy it is to bust a car window? How fast it can be done? A ten year old can do it in less than six seconds! And a poor cop has another larceny from auto on his hands. Another crime to write a report on, waste another half hour on. Another crime to make him look bad.

Meanwhile, the idiot who left the family heirlooms on the back seat in the first place is raising hell about where were the cops when the car was being looted. He's planning to write letters to the mayor and police commissioner about what a lousy police force you have here; they can't even keep my car from getting ripped off! What, were they drinking coffee somewhere?

And the cops are saying to themselves, Let me tell you, jerk-weed, we were seven blocks away, taking another stupid report from another idiot civilian about his stupid car being broken into because he left his stuff on the back seat too.

These civilians can't figure out that maybe they shouldn't leave stuff [lying] around unattended where anybody can just pick it up and boogie.

Maybe they should put the stuff in the trunk, where no one but Superman is gonna see it. Maybe they should do that before they get to where they're going, just in case some riffraff is hanging around watching them while the car is being secured.

Another thing that drives cops wild is the *"surely this doesn't apply to me"* syndrome, which never fails to reveal itself at scenes of sniper or barricade incidents.

There's always some idiot walking down the street (or jogging or driving) who thinks the police cars blocking off the area, the ropes marked POLICE LINE: DO NOT CROSS, the cops crouched behind cars pointing revolvers, carbines, shotguns, and bazookas at some building, all of this has nothing whatsoever to do with him—so he weasels around the barricades or slithers under the restraining ropes and blithely continues on his way, right into the line of fire.

The result is that some cop risks his ass (or hers—don't forget, the cops include women now) to go after the cretin, and drag him, usually under protest, back to safety.

All of these cops, including the one risking his ass, devoutly hope that the sniper will get off one miraculous shot and drill the idiot right between the horns, which would have two immediate effects:

The quiche for brains civilian would be dispatched to the next world, and every cop on the scene would instantaneously be licensed to kill the scumbag doing the sniping. Whereupon the cops would destroy the whole freaking building, sniper and all, in about 30 seconds, which is what they wanted to do in the first place, except the brass wouldn't let them because the idiot hadn't killed anybody yet.

An allied phenomenon is the *"my isn't this amusing"* behavior exhibited, usually by Yuppies or other members of high society, at some emergency scenes. For example, a group of trendy types will be strolling down the street when a squad car with lights flashing and siren on screeches up to a building. They'll watch the cops yank out their guns and run up to the door, flatten themselves against the wall and peep into the place cautiously. Now if you think about it, something serious could be happening here. Cops usually don't pull their revolvers to go get a cup of coffee. They usually don't hug the sides of buildings just before dropping in to say hello.

Any five year old ghetto kid can tell you these cops are definitely ready to cap somebody. But do our society friends perceive this? Do they stay out of the cops' way? Of course not! They think it's vastly amusing. And of course, since they're not involved in the funny little game the cops are playing, they think nothing can happen to them.

While the ghetto kid is hiding behind a car waiting for the shooting to start, *Muffy, Chip, and Biffy* are continuing their stroll, right up to the officers, tittering among themselves about how silly the cops look, all scrunched up against the wall, trying to look in through the door without stopping bullets with their foreheads.

What the cops are hoping, at this point, is for a homicidal holdup man to come busting out the door with a sawed-off shotgun. They're hoping he has it loaded with elephant shot, and that he immediately identifies our socialites as serious threats to his personal well-being. They're hoping he has just enough ammunition to blast the hell out of the gigglers, but not enough to return fire when the cops open up on him.

Of course if that actually happens, the poor cops will be in a world of trouble for not protecting the *"innocent bystanders."* The brass wouldn't even want to hear that the idiots probably didn't have enough sense to come in out of an acid rain. Somebody ought to tell the quiche eaters out there to stand back when they encounter someone with a gun in his hand, whether he happens to be wearing a badge or a ski mask.

Civilians also aggravate cops in a number of other ways. One of their favorite games is, "Officer can you tell me . . . ?" A cop knows he's been selected to play this game whenever someone approaches and utters those magic words. Now it's okay if they continue with, ". . . how to get to so and so street?" or ". . . where such and such a place is located?" After all, cops should be familiar with the area in which they work. But it eats the lining of their stomachs when some idiot asks, "Where can I catch the fifty-four bus?" Or, "Where can I find a telephone?"

Cops look forward to their last day before retirement, when they can safely give these idiots the answer they've been choking back for 20 years: *"No maggot,* I can't tell ya where the fifty-four bus runs! What does this look like, an MTA uniform? Go ask a bus driver! And no, *dog breath,* I don't know where ya can find a phone, except wherever your eyes see one! Take your head out of your ass and look for one!"

And cops just love to find a guy parking his car in a crosswalk next to a fire hydrant at a bus stop posted with a sign saying, *"Don't Even Think About Stopping, Standing, or Parking Here. Cars Towed Away, Forfeited to the Government, and Sold at Public Auction,"* and the jerk asks, *"Officer, may I park here a minute?"*

"What are ya nuts? Of course ya can park here. As long as ya like! Leave it all day! Ya don't see anything that says ya can't, do ya? You're welcome. See ya later." The cop then drives around the corner and calls for a tow truck to remove the vehicle.

Later, in traffic court, the idiot will be whining to the judge, "But your honor, I asked an officer if I could park there, and he said I could! No I don't know which officer, but I did ask! Honest! No wait judge, I can't afford five hundred dollars! This isn't fair! I'm not creating a disturbance! I've got rights! Get your hands off me! Where are you taking me? What do you mean ten days for contempt of court? What did I do? Wait, wait . . ." If you should happen to see a cop humming contentedly and smiling to himself for no apparent reason, he may have won this game.

Wildly, *unrealistic civilian expectations* also contribute to a cop's distaste for the general citizenry. An officer can be running his ass off all day or night, handling call after call and writing volumes of police reports, but everybody thinks their problem is the only thing he has to work on.

The policeman may have a few worries too. Ever think of that? The sergeant is on him because he's been late for roll call a few days; he's been battling like a badger with his wife, who's just about to leave him because he never takes her anywhere and doesn't spend enough time at home and the kids need braces and the station wagon needs a major engine overhaul and where are we going to get the money to pay for all that and we haven't had a real vacation for years and all you do is hang around with other cops and you've been drinking too much lately and I could've married that wonderful guy I was going with when I met you and lived happily ever after and why don't you get a regular job with regular days off and no night shifts and decent pay and a chance for advancement and no one throwing bottles or taking wild potshots at you?

Meanwhile, that sweet young thing he met on a call last month says her period is late. Internal Affairs is investigating him on a disorderly arrest last week; the captain is pissed at him for tagging a councilman's car; a burglar's tearing up the businesses on his post; and he's already handled two robberies, three family fights, a stolen auto, and a half dozen juvenile complaints today.

Now here he is on another juvenile call, trying to explain to some bimbo, who's president of her neighborhood improvement association, that the security of western civilization is not really threatened all that much by the kids who hang around on the corner by her house.

"Yes officer, I know they're not there now. They always leave whenever you come by. But right after you're gone, they come right back, don't you see, and continue their disturbance. It's intolerable! I'm so upset, I can barely sleep at night!"

By now the cop's eyes have glazed over. "What we need here officer," she continues vehemently, "is greater attention to this matter by the police. You and some other officers should hide and stake out that corner so those renegades wouldn't see you. Then you could catch them in the act!"

"Yes ma'am, we'd love to stake out that corner a few hours every night, since we don't have anything else to do, but I've got a better idea," he'd like to say. "Here's a box of fragmentation grenades the Department obtained from the army just for situations like this. The next time you see those little crumb snatchers out there, just lob a couple of these into the crowd and get down!"

Or he's got an artsy-craftsy type who's just moved into a tough, rundown neighborhood and decides it's gotta be cleaned up. You know, *"Urban Pioneers."*

The cops see a lot of them now. The cops call them volunteer victims. Most of them are intelligent, talented, hard-working, well-paid folks with masochistic chromosomes interspersed among their otherwise normal genes. They have nice jobs, live in nice homes, and have a lot of nice material possessions, and they somehow decide that it would be just a marvelous idea to move into a slum and get yoked, roped, looted, and pillaged on a regular basis.

What else do they expect? Peace and harmony? It's like tossing a juicy little pig into a piranha tank.

Moving day: Here come the pioneers, dropping all their groovy gear from their Volvo station wagon, setting it on the sidewalk so everyone on the block can get a good look at the food processor, the microwave, the stereo system, the color TV, the tape deck, etc.

At the same time, the local burglars are appraising the goods, unofficially, and calculating how much they can get for the TV down at the corner bar, how much the stereo will bring at Joe's Garage, who might want the tape deck at the barbershop, and maybe mama can use the microwave herself.

When the pioneers get ripped off, the cops figure they asked for it, and they got it. You want to poke your arm in a tiger cage? Don't be amazed when he eats it for lunch. The cops regard it as naive for *trendies* to move into crime zones and conduct their lives the same way they did up on *Society Hill.*

In fact, they can't fathom why anyone who didn't have to would want to move there at all, regardless of how they want to live or how prepared they might be to adapt their behavior.

That's probably because the cops are intimately acquainted with all those petty but disturbing crimes and nasty little incidents that never make the newspapers but profoundly [affect] the quality of life in a particular area.

Something else that causes premature aging among cops is the "I don't know who to call, so I'll call the police" ploy.

Why, the cops ask themselves, do they get so many calls for things like water leaks, sick cases, bats in houses, and the like—things that have nothing whatsoever to do with law enforcement or the maintenance of public order?

They figure it's because civilians are getting more and more accustomed to having the government solving problems for them, and the local P.D. is the only government agency that'll even answer the phone at 3:00 A.M., let alone send anybody.

So when the call comes over the radio to go to such-and-such an address for a water leak, the assigned officer rolls his eyes, acknowledges, responds, surveys the problem, and tells the complainant, "Yep, that's a water leak all right! No doubt about it. Ya oughta call a plumber! And it might not be a bad idea to turn off your main valve for [a while]." Or, "Yep, your Aunt Minnie's sick all right! Ya probably oughta get'er to a doctor tomorrow if she doesn't get any better by then." Or, "Yep, that's a bat all right! Maybe ya oughta open the windows so it can fly outside again!"

In the meantime, while our hero is wasting time on this nothing call, maybe somebody is having a real problem out there, like getting raped, robbed, or killed.

Street cops would like to work the phones just once and catch a few of these idiotic complaints: "A bat in your house? No need to send an officer when I can tell ya what to do right here on the phone, pal! Close all your doors and windows right away. Pour gasoline all over your furniture. That's it. Now set it on fire and get everybody outside! Yeah, you'll get that little critter for sure! That's okay; call us anytime."

Probably the most serious beef cops have with civilians relates to those situations in which the use of force becomes necessary to deal with some desperado who may have just robbed a bank, iced somebody, beat up his wife and kids, or wounded some cop, and now he's caught, but won't give up.

He's not going to be taken alive, he's going to take some cops with him, and you better say your prayers, you pig. Naturally, if the chump's armed with any kind of weapon, the cops are going to shoot the crap out of him so bad they'll be able to open up his body later as a lead mine.

If he's not armed, and the cops aren't creative enough to find a weapon for him, they'll just beat him into raw meat and hope he spends the [next] few weeks in traction.

They view it as a learning experience for the moron. You mess up somebody, you find out what it feels like to get messed up. Don't like it? Don't do it again! It's called "street justice," and civilians approve of it as much as cops do—even if they don't admit it.

Remember how the audience cheered when Charles Bronson messed up the bad guys in Death Wish?

How they scream with joy every time Clint Eastwood's Dirty Harry makes his day by blowing up some rotten scumball with his .44 magnum?

What they applaud is the administration of street justice. The old eye-for-an-eye concept, one of mankind's most primal instincts.

All of us have it, especially cops.

It severely offends and deeply hurts cops when they administer a dose of *good old-fashioned street justice* only to have some bleeding-heart do-gooder happen upon the scene at the last minute, when the hairbag is at last getting his just desserts, and start hollering about police brutality.

Cops regard that as very serious business indeed. Brutality can get them fired. Get fired from one police department, and it's tough to get a job as a cop anywhere else ever again.

Brutality exposes the cop to civil liability as well, also, his superior officers, the police department as an agency, and maybe even the local government itself.

You've seen 60 Minutes, right? Some cop screws up, gets sued along with everybody else in the department who ever had anything to do with him, and the city or county ends up paying the plaintiff umpty-ump million dollars, raising taxes and hocking its fire engines in the process.

What do you think happens to the cop who screwed up in the first place? He's done for.

On many occasions when the cops are accused of excessive force, the apparent brutality is a misperception by some observer who isn't acquainted with the realities of police work.

For example, do you have any idea how hard it is to handcuff someone who really doesn't want to be handcuffed? Without hurting them? It's almost impossible for one cop to accomplish by himself unless he beats the hell out of the prisoner first—which would also be viewed as brutality!

It frequently takes three or four cops to handcuff one son of a b&^%h who's absolutely determined to battle them.

In situations like that, it's not unusual for the cops to hear someone in the crowd of onlookers comment on how they're ganging up on the poor b#@*ard, and beating him unnecessarily.

This makes them feel like telling the complainer, "*Hey idiot,* you think you can handcuff this unruly by yourself without killing him first? C'mere! You're deputized! Now, go ahead and do it!"

The problem is that, in addition to being unfamiliar with how difficult it is in the real world to physically control someone without beating his ass, last minute observers usually don't have the opportunity to see for themselves, like they do in the movies and on TV, what a monster the suspect might be.

If they did, they'd probably holler at the cops to beat his ass some more. They might even want to help!

The best thing for civilians to do if they see the cops rough up somebody too much is to keep their mouths shut at the scene, and to make inquires of the police brass later on.

There might be ample justification for the degree of force used that just wasn't apparent at the time of the arrest. If not, the brass will be very interested in the complaint. If one of their cops went over the deep end, they'll want to know about it.

Most of this comes down to common sense, a characteristic the cops feel most civilians lack. One of the elements of common sense is thinking before opening one's yap or taking other action.

Just a brief moment of thought will often prevent the utterance of something stupid or the commission of idiotic acts that will, among other things, generate nothing but contempt from the average street cop.

Think—and it might mean getting a warning instead of a traffic ticket. Or getting sent on your way rather than being arrested.

Or continuing on to your original destination instead of to the hospital. It might mean getting some real assistance instead of the run-around. The very least it'll get you is a measure of respect cops seldom show civilians.

Act like you've got just a little sense, and even if the cops don't like you, they at least *won't hate you.*

That is the end of the article, and I am not going to make any comment at this point. Either you are laughing and picking up some ideas to make your life easier, or you're having a complete breakdown.

CHAPTER

30

# OUTSIDE SUPPORTS FOR LAW ENFORCEMENT

# SEE SOMETHING, SAY SOMETHIING

Your police department will depend upon a host of support personnel. The obvious ones are those civilians who work with you in your police station. They are here to support your mission and are a vital part of the overall operation.

When you call your police station whom, or should I say **what**, greets you, most likely, it is a machine listing numerous options. The first option is always 9-1-1 to ensure the municipality is legally covered. Our old city manager Paul Lemont vowed that we would never lose this personal service to the public. He was a good manager and maintained it for years, but through time, some slick salespeople, and the budget crunchers, we now have a machine being the first contact with the police department. I'm sure this is the case in most police departments. Most of us understand the 9-1-1 calling system for emergencies. I certainly hope this is still taught in our school systems. I have not called 9-1-1 in many years, but I assume this still goes directly to a person. That said, I am sure there is some pencil pusher out there, sponsored by some software provider, trying to automate this. Not every call made to a police department, however, is an emergency, but often they are urgent enough to avoid the long list of options we so often get. In response to ongoing terrorist activities, **"See something, say something"** is the phrase promoted for the average citizen to report suspicious activity. For the person who wanted to provide a quick tip, maybe reluctantly, are they going to listen to the minute- or two-minute-long menu before they can **"SAY SOMETHING"**? Or are they going to be directed to another machine with a new set of menu options? Your police department should have qualified **PEOPLE**, also known as human beings, initially answering the phones. It's good for the employment rate, it's good for your department, and it's good for public safety.

When I first came on the job in 1979, there was great debate about having civilians performing the jobs that police officers once performed. Most notably was the position of dispatcher. Although there were arguments, both pro and con, I can say after my years of experience that dispatchers are a separate and unique profession. That's not to say an officer can't learn these skills, nor should they be excluded from temporarily filling in (minutes, not days). But such as the job is, dispatchers need to be focused on gaining experience in that profession. I had the pleasure of working with dozens of professional dispatchers over the years. One part of the training for dispatchers that I strongly recommend is occasionally having them spend time on the road with an officer as they are patrolling. It will give them great insight into how they can better serve the officers and realize how quickly time goes by when you are in the middle of a crisis.

There will be numerous other support personnel within your department—IT technicians, clerical staff, secretarial staff, custodians, etc. They are usually the people who put all the pieces of your operation together and make if functional. Oftentimes these people are the first contact many citizens have with the police department. It is imperative that you hire qualified support personnel. It is also imperative to do thorough background checks on these employees as well. They are going to have access to a lot of sensitive information, even if you don't intend them to. They are going to be seeing the confidential reports lying out on your desk and the data being entered and available in your database. They are going to be seeing that confidential informant you secretly let in the back door. Make sure your support staff is trustworthy.

Who are the support people you need from outside your department? The list is long, but if you are going to function efficiently in your job, you need to foster relationships with these people. I will mention some of the more obvious here.

First is obviously our cousins in the fire and EMS services—cousins, not brothers and sisters, because they get to officially sleep after midnight. You are going to be working side by side with these people every day, and a good relationship will go a long way. I can't tell you how many times we helped firefighters perform their tasks and, likewise, the times they came to our aid. There was never a lot of "not my job" exchanges as we all knew that we were there for the public good and that we all wanted to go home that night in the same condition as we came to work. More than once, I saw a firefighter jumping in to help us restrain a combatant in the middle of a brawl. I specifically remember one time in Riverside when "Robin Hood" was shooting arrows from his balcony. The firefighters were right there beside me as we rushed him while he renocked his bow.

Second, public works and the building inspectors are a great asset. Not all your problems can be fixed with traditional law enforcement methods. Crime tends to flourish in run-down neighborhoods, so be a problem solver and do something to fix it. These inspectors should be made aware of these issues. A building inspector shuttering a building because it is unsafe is a great way to help solve some of the issues you are trying to resolve.

Attorneys are going to be a part of your career. It is obvious why you want to have a good relationship with the attorneys in the prosecutor's office. You need them to prosecute not only your criminal cases but also your relationship, especially when working in specialized units, should be that you can call upon them for advice as you proceed with your investigation. In Rhode Island, we had the Office of Attorney General. You could always reach out to one of the staff and get assistance regardless of the day or time. Our own solicitor at the time, Robert Nocera, Esq., was a great instructor. Prior to every case being presented at court, he would sit and review it with us. By the end of the review, you would feel there was no way we could win, but then he would go into action in the court. It was truly amazing to see him secure conviction after conviction. He was the reason we had one of, if not the best, drunk-driving conviction rates in the state of Rhode Island. He took the time to train us in each element that was needed. Even the defense attorneys who specialized in drunk-driving cases were reluctant to take on a case when they realized it was brought by East Providence.

Defense lawyers are another group you are going to be dealing with on a regular basis, and when possible, you should have a good relationship with them as well. There are a few rogue defense lawyers out there who hate police officers, but the majority of them are simply doing their job. Don't hate them as they are just a part of our wonderful judicial system, and as a police officer, you may likely need one of them someday. Stand for your case but don't personalize it. Except as mentioned above, they are not your enemy. If you treat them as an enemy (compared with an adversary), there may be a day you are standing in the witness box and your "enemy" is the one questioning you.

When court takes a recess, sit and have a coffee with them. Even if their client is with them and they invite you to join them, join them. When you see them out in public, invite them to join you. You might be amazed at what they teach you about how to better prepare a case the next time. We had one of the most noted organized crime attorneys spend time, teaching us how to better prepare a case while at the police academy. His lessons were genuine. As participants in a competitive interaction, a good defense lawyer wants a good opponent. It was very rewarding when after a session of cross-examination, the defense lawyer would approach you and commend you on your testimony. This is also the place where your credibility comes into account. If a lawyer knows you are a person of integrity, you may very well avoid some of the frivolous complaints being sought by their clients.

The operators of the local tow company are another group of people you should have a good relationship with. If you have an active department, you are going to be towing cars, and you need to know you can trust the people doing the work. It also comes in handy if you decide to explore some unchartered region of your beat some night and get stuck up to the doors in mud. If you have a relationship with your tow operator and know of a twenty-four-hour car wash, you may save yourself some unnecessary paperwork.

Amendment I of the United States Constitution provides for a free press. Law enforcement, in general, seems to have a dislike of the press, sometimes for a good cause, and is certainly portrayed as a fact throughout the world of television. Reporters are there, always asking questions about what the police department is doing and for a good reason. Part of a free country is keeping government accountable, and you as a police officer are a part of the government. There are things you should share with the press and other things, such as aspects of ongoing investigations, you should not. If you establish a good rapport with the reporters you deal with, treat them with respect and share what is appropriate. They are likely going to respect you for your actions. Even if they come upon some information from another source, if you have this relationship, they may—but they don't have to—hold parts of the story back to not impede your investigation. If you constantly give the reporters a hard time and are always making the statement "no comment," if they are good reporters, they are going to keep digging. If you keep obstructing a good reporter, there may come a time when you regret this. Be it right or wrong, a reporter who does not have a good impression of you may very well put a spin on a story someday, which is not beneficial to you or your department.

Administrators need to set up guidelines on how your department will deal with the press. Administrators should not be the camera hogs and be the only face the public associates with the police department. Let the officers actually involved in the investigation provide the information. If they are not "camera worthy," teach them to become so. It's interesting to see how in those departments that constantly boast about community policing just how much delegation is actually given to officers when it comes to speaking with the press. These departments are supposedly working in an environment that does not require a lot of direction from the main office. A press release by the officers in this delegated role should be no different than that of allowing them to take other actions, without hierarchal authority. If you truly believe in this policy, then adhere to it.

In summation, as a police officer, your support base consists of many people, not just the ones mentioned above. The relationship you have with the butcher, the baker, the candlestick maker, etc., is going to determine how well you are going to function as a law enforcement officer in your community.

# RETIREMENT

## IT'S NOT THE END

Hopefully, you will not be killed in the line of duty, and you will be able to retire at the end of your career. When you retire, enjoy yourself; you earned it. Capt. William Callaghan sent me the quote below shortly before my retirement, and it sums up the retirement of a law enforcement officer so well.

### WHEN COPS RETIRE

When a good man leaves "the job" and retires to a better life, many are jealous, some are pleased and yet others, who may have already retired, wonder. We wonder if [they] know what they are leaving behind, because we already know. We know for example that after a lifetime of camaraderie that few experience, it will remain as a longing for those past times. We know in the law enforcement life there is a fellowship which lasts long after the uniforms are hung up in the back of the closet. We know even if he throws them away, they will be on him with every step and breath that remains in his frame. We also know how the very bearing of the man or woman speaks of what he/she was and, in his or her heart, still is. These are the burdens of the job. You will still look at people suspiciously, still see what others do not see or

choose to ignore and always will look at the rest of the
law enforcement world with a respect for what they do;
only grown in a lifetime of knowing. Never think for
one moment you are escaping from the life. You are only
escaping "the job" and we are merely allowing you to leave
"active" duty.

So what I wish for you is that whenever you ease into
retirement, in your heart you never forget for one moment
that "Blessed are the Peacemakers for they shall be called
children of God," (Romans 13:1–4) and you are still a
member of the greatest fraternity the world has ever
known.

When I retired, I remember how sad I was on my last day, just before
my last roll call. I sat in Chief Norman Miranda's office, actually crying
for a period. It seemed as if the world I had known for years was coming
to an end. Why? Because it was. On the other side of this reaction, there
are those officers who look at that last day with great anticipation and can't
wait to get out the door and enjoy retirement. Regardless of where officers
fit into this range of emotions, we all still and will feel very connected to
law enforcement once we leave. The key in your retirement is to move on
doing something. Many take up an alternative career in law enforcement,
while some take up completely different careers, totally unrelated to law
enforcement. Some truly retire and enjoy all the recreational activities they
can fit into a day every day. I know when I was asked what I do for a living,
the first line is "I'm a retired police officer," followed by the job I am actually
doing at the time. As the quote above states, you are always part of the law
enforcement family, and those memories will always be a part of your life.

I encourage my sister and brother officers to stay active once you retire.
Most of us have earned a nice pension, but it is even better if you get to
stick around for a while and actually get to enjoy it. There seemed to be
two ends of this spectrum. Some officers, shortly after retirement, pass on.
Others seem to just keep on going. I believe the key to longevity is to be
engaged in something.

Although you will be a cop forever, you can't always rely on this to be
your identity in life. The fifty-year-old who was once the high school star
athlete and still clings to this status for their identity is missing out in
life. The past molded you, but it should not define who you are now. You

can keep your identity as a law enforcement officer but reinvent yourself. Continue to support those officers doing the job from your position as a civilian. Unfortunately, sometimes they cannot make the statements that you now can. Simply put, who cares whom you upset? They can't fire you, and you have your pension. So stick up for those officers who might not be able to speak their mind in the public sphere. For you young officers, make sure that you respect those who came before you and made your job safer through their sacrifices. Keep your retired officers in the loop so they can support you when needed. Most retired officers will gladly do whatever they can to support the mission of law enforcement.

Before you retire, have a plan in place for your retirement years. To all my brothers and sisters, thank you for your years of service.

Fifteen years retired, and it still fits . . . barely.

# CHAPTER 32

# CORRECTIONS

What do you call a public servant who wears a uniform and is issued a shield, a firearm, a baton, and handcuffs? These public servants also have the authority to arrest people and petition the courts for an arrest warrant. They are also patrolling on a daily basis, looking for criminal activity, and maintaining order. My guess is the word that comes first to your mind is not *guard*. They are correctional OFFICERS. They do the same thing police officers do, only their beat is much smaller and much more dangerous.

I realize that the field of corrections is different from police work, but is it really that different? Obviously, I am biased based on my daughter's experience as a correctional officer and the support her family received from the community of correctional officers upon her death, but I would ask you consider how important their role is in the criminal justice system and to treat them with the respect they deserve as fellow officers.

As police officers, most of the people we interact with on a daily basis are not criminals. Correctional officers, on the other hand, are dealing mostly with a lot of criminals on a daily basis. It is a grueling job with a lot of pressure. The last thing these officers need is to be disrespected by police officers. We catch the criminals, but they have to deal with them daily. How well they do with the incarcerated will affect our lives once these individuals return to society.

We must also consider the term *corrections*. The goal of the correction's system, for the most part, is to rehabilitate criminals. My coworker Capt. Joseph Broadmeadow made a great observation about this topic in one of his articles: "We cannot expect a prison system that amounts to nothing more than a warehouse of troubled humans to return a better person back to society."

How true. I believe there is hope for the rehabilitation of a good portion of the people who enter our corrections system if the right programs are in place. On the other hand, there is a group of people who are so evil and demented that they should never see the light of day. These violent career criminals should not be placed in with the general population so that they can influence and prey upon the weaker inmates. They need to be isolated and secured and, in some cases, executed. For those of you who are against capital punishment, you need to provide me with an alternative. First, don't pull your dusty Bible off the shelf for this one issue and say it is prohibited. Quite the contrary. Now I would like an explanation what should happen to a prisoner when he kills a correctional officer. The prisoner is already serving four consecutive life sentences for raping, murdering, and cannibalizing four innocent people. What possible deterrent is there for him not to kill a correctional officer, just for the sport of it? There are many incarcerated criminals who fit this mold and worse. What is your remedy for this dilemma? Give him another life sentence? Take away his television and teddy bear? If you have a viable solution other than capital punishment, I would gladly listen. Capital punishment is needed to provide the protection our correctional officers deserve, let alone the rest of us, from these monsters.

That is all I am going to say about corrections, but remember, correctional officers work the toughest beat in the country, and they deserve our respect.

### "CORRECTIONS, NO GUNS, JUST GUTS!"

# MEMORABLE QUOTES
# FROM MY CAREER

I have been forwarded many statements, blurbs, and the like during my career as well as since I retired. Some of these I have saved and would like to share with you, the reader of this book. I don't know the original author on most. At the end of this chapter are numerous quotes from some of my coworkers. Only a few know who made the statement, and that is how we will leave it.

As a Christian, the Bible has had a great influence on my life, including my career as a police officer. Some of these verses, I think, are very applicable to law enforcement.

> Every person is to be in subjection to the governing authorities. For there is no authority except from God, and those which exist are established by God. Therefore whoever resists authority has opposed the ordinance of God; and they who have opposed will receive condemnation upon themselves. For rulers are not a cause of fear for good behavior, but for evil. Do you want to have no fear of authority? Do what is good and you will have praise from the same; for it is a minister of God to you for good. But if you do what is evil, be afraid; for it does not bear the sword for nothing; for it is a minister of God, an avenger who brings wrath on the one who practices evil. (Romans 13:1–4, NASB)

As a commander, I would use the above verses for counseling when an officer was involved in the death of a suspect. Contrary to popular belief, whenever a law enforcement officer takes the life of another in the performance of their duty, it has a great impact on them, and that officer needs counseling and support. That is a part of your job as a supervisor.

> This is My commandment, that you love one another, just as I have loved you. Greater love has no one than this, that one lay down his life for his friends. (John 15:12–13, NASB)

I think this is pretty self-explanatory when it comes to the fact that police officers put their lives on the line every day to protect not only their friends but also citizens whom they do not know. They go above and beyond, and they should be honored for this sacrifice.

Below is a blurb I received from someone at some point in my life. The source is not important, but the content of the comparison is spot on, so I thought it was worth saving and now sharing.

### CIVILIAN FRIENDS VERSUS POLICE FRIENDS

**CIVILIAN FRIENDS** get upset if you're too busy to talk to them for a week.

**POLICE FRIENDS** are glad to see you after years and will happily carry on the same conversation you were having last time you met.

**CIVILIAN FRIENDS** never ask for food or alcohol.

**POLICE FRIENDS** are the reason you have no food or alcohol.

**CIVILIAN FRIENDS** call your parents mister and missus.

**POLICE FRIENDS** call your parents mom and dad.

**CIVILIAN FRIENDS** bail you out of jail and tell you what you did was wrong.

**POLICE FRIENDS** would be sitting next to you in jail, saying, "Damn . . . we screwed up . . . but man, that was fun!"

**CIVILIAN FRIENDS** have never seen you cry.

**POLICE FRIENDS** cry with you.

**CIVILIAN FRIENDS** borrow your stuff for a few days then give it back.

**POLICE FRIENDS** keep your stuff so long, they forget it's yours.

**CIVILIAN FRIENDS** know a few things about you.

**POLICE FRIENDS** could write a book with direct quotes from you.

**CIVILIAN FRIENDS** will leave you behind if that's what the crowd is doing.

**POLICE FRIENDS** will kick the whole crowd's ass who left you behind.

**CIVILIAN FRIENDS** would knock on your door.

**POLICE FRIENDS** walk right in and say, "I'm home!"

**CIVILIAN FRIENDS** are for a while.

**POLICE FRIENDS** are for life.

**CIVILIAN FRIENDS** have shared a few experiences.

**POLICE FRIENDS** have shared a lifetime of experiences no citizen could ever dream of.

**CIVILIAN FRIENDS** will talk crap to the person who talks crap about you.

**POLI CE FRIENDS** will knock them the hell out for using your name in vain.

**CIVILIAN FRIENDS** will ignore this.

**POLICE FRIENDS** will forward this.

Most police officers will have a good, albeit a little twisted at times, sense of humor. I believe this is a coping system we use to deal with all the horror and evil we see on a regular basis. If you are not part of this family, you might not appreciate it, but it exists. I will take credit for the next story.

At one point, I was selected to represent the state's police chiefs in a multidepartment group to assist the state attorney general in preparing a standardized evidence manual that was going to deal with all aspects of evidence and property seized by the state through criminal investigations. Of the seven people there, most were high-ranking assistant directors from various state agencies. The only one I knew was the assistant district attorney (ADA). The topic came up about destroying seized firearms when I interjected and stated, **"You mean we have to destroy them? We usually auction them off a few times a years to raise money for equipment."**

The room was dead silent for a good thirty seconds. I kept my poker face, while their faces looked as if they had just seen a ghost until the ADA. finally asked, **"Roger, please tell me you're joking."**

**"Of course,"** I replied. The sigh of relief that was now on their faces was priceless.

For the following quotes, **99.999 percent** of the people who will read these will have no idea what they mean or who said them. Actually, 90 percent of the officers I worked with will not know them all. These quotes will not be standing the test of time; however, the quotes were so memorable at the time they were uttered that they just needed to be put to paper. For those of you who recognize the moment, I hope you enjoy the humorous memory.

1. **"Hold that 'R' 'F' there. I am two clicks and a mike away."**
2. **"I am so high, I could hunt ducks with a ball-peen hammer."**
3. **"I don't care. Is he breathing?"**
4. **"We haven't had a good firefight in a while."**
5. **"Hey, guys, you want to hear a tape from a firefight I made in Nam? Automatic weapons fire, pretty cool."**

6. "World War III is going to start in the trunk of your cruiser."
7. Sergeant radios, "S-1, 10-80 (a vehicle pursuit)!" Dispatcher asks, "Description of the car, Sergeant?" Sergeant replies, "Fast, very f——ing fast!"
8. "Okay, guys, where did you toss the blackjacks?"
9. "Big Eddy."
10. "Did you guys ever hear a grenade simulator go off?" (As the pin is pulled out of a grenade, it is tossed about twenty yards away—a moment you will always remember.)
11. "Moose, tug, rhino."
12. "All 4-12 cars. You can respond to the bar fight, but no overtime slips and NO prisoners!"
13. "Pick up —— at the Saxony lounge." (This was one of the most dreaded assignments of all.)
14. "Trembles."
15. "Ski, going to the palms?"
16. "Don't worry. He's faking it."
17. "Sorry, Lieutenant. He's dead."
18. "Are we really going to wait for SWAT? Let's not become a bunch of wimps. Kick that door in. Let's go."
19. "Hey, are you okay?" (Slurred response) "Yeah, I was cutting the grass, and I wiped my head with the wrong rag. It was full of gasoline."
20. "Red alert!"
21. "Beansie."
22. "You know, Chief, speaking of getting a new attitude, I went to the attitude store today, but they were fresh out of new ones."
23. "The white glove society."
24. "Hey, pal. Let me tell you that's one hell of a grip you got."
25. "Hey, I have a special Christmas cookie here. It was made especially for you."
26. "Hey, buddy. Are you a *Homo sapiens?*"
27. Master of ceremonies at a retirement party says, "Then he found baby Jesus." The crowd immediately laughs. It is interrupted immediately by the emcee. "Don't laugh," the emcee says. "You better thank God he did because let me tell you . . .'"
28. Arresting officer 1 says to arresting officer 2 (prior to *spell check*), "Hey, how do you spell Quaaludes?" The person under arrest responds, "Q-U-A-A-L-U-D-E-S."

29. "I can't believe that light is still on after all that!"

30. Detectives would prepare a "photo pack" consisting of six photographs that would allow victims and witnesses to pick out and positively identify the suspect from a group of people. The state prosecutor says, "Detective, it appears there are three different photographs of the same person in this photo pack?" The detective replies, "Yes, you are correct. I didn't want them to miss the guilty party."

31. Yelling "Roll the window down before you puke out of it!"

CHAPTER

34

# CONCLUSION

I chose this last chapter to relay some random thoughts as they come to mind. I have been working on this for years, and I decided that it is time to get it out for others to read, and hopefully, it has a positive impact on law enforcement.

Currently and most certainly, there have been and will be periods in our culture where the police are despised by certain groups. As a law enforcement officer, you have to take the high ground and not let emotions rule your actions. As a citizen, don't join the herd of lemmings and run over the cliff. Please use rational thought and make educated decisions. Oftentimes the people behind this hatred would love a society where their criminal actions can flourish in an environment where the police are constantly being second-guessed, and, worse, second-guessing themselves. I saw one year in a neighboring city where public scrutiny was way beyond what it should have been. As a result of this, the police felt handcuffed, and unfortunately, the murder rate soared, most often young children falling victim to street crime. Police officers don't have the luxury of working in an environment where everything is black and white, and I am not referring to race.

I do not excuse poor or unlawful actions by police officers. If you think such things are taking place in your community, have the courage to report it to the proper authorities. Get it resolved. Don't add to a problem that may already exist by hate rants and the like, which do not only solve the problem but also exacerbate it by alienating and endangering those officers who are risking their lives every day to make you safe.

If you are thinking of a career in law enforcement, please make sure you are considering this for the right reasons. Your first reason needs to be that you want to be a good servant to the public. Yes, there are great benefits, but there are also great dangers. If you are in law enforcement, be the best police officer you can be. If you are a citizen, support your police whenever you can. This will make their mission easier, and the result is your community be safer and you will live in a way that so many have fought to preserve.

> We hold these truths to be self-evident, that all men are created equal, that they are endowed by their Creator with certain unalienable rights that among these are **Life**, **Liberty** and the pursuit of **Happiness**.

In closing, I want to thank God for having the privilege of serving as a public servant in accordance with the book of Romans 13. I want to thank my family for always supporting me throughout my career, which was not always easy on them, especially my children Randy, Kimberly, Amanda, and Roger III. I am also grateful to all my brother and sister officers whom I have had the honor to work with over the years. Thank you for being there for me and putting your life on the line to protect me as well as others.